PORTUGAL
Gail Aguiar, Jenny Barchfield, Austin Bush,
Daniel James Clarke, Sandra Henriques,
Marlene Marques, Joana Taborda

Meet our writers

JUAMPITER/GETTY IMAGES ©

Gail Aguiar

@gailatlarge

Gail is a Philippines-born, Canadian-raised content maker living in Porto since 2013. After decades of moving her home base, she's happily settled into a photographer's paradise complete with flaky pastries, striking architecture and sun-dried laundry.

Jenny Barchfield

A native of Tucson, Arizona, Jenny attended Barnard College and Columbia University before embarking on a life abroad. She worked as a foreign correspondent for a major newswire, first in Paris, where she covered breaking news as well as the culture beat, and then in Rio de Janeiro. Jenny moved to Lisbon in 2017.

Austin Bush

@bushaustin

After more than two decades of living in Thailand, Austin moved to Portugal in 2022. He is happiest nibbling olives and sipping wine, and is grateful for a life that involves much less sweating.

Daniel James Clarke

@danflyingsolo and @guide2portugal

Dorset-born Daniel's first zest for Portugal was aged five, when a kind-faced farmer handed him an Algarvian orange, a story that blossomed into a relocation. Writing and photographing across the globe, Dan has turned his passion for travel into a job.

Previous spread Douro Valley (p202)

KERRY MURRAY/LONELY PLANET ©

Reserva Natural de Berlenga
Parque Natural das Serras de Aire e Candeeiros
Abrantes
Óbidos
Lisbon 1 hr
Río Tejo
Portalegre
Parque Natural da Serra de São Mamede
SPAIN
Beyond Lisbon 82
Alentejo 108
Elvas
Estremoz
Lisbon 48
Porto 4.5 hrs
Setúbal
Faro 2.5 hrs
Évora
Sines
Beja
Río Sado
Río Guadiana
Parque Natural do Vale do Guadiana
Parque Natural do Sudoeste Alentejano e Costa Vicentina
The Algarve 136
Costa Vicentina 134
Lagos
Albufeira
Faro
Golfo de Cádiz
Parque Natural da Ria Formosa

WARRE'S

Bury your feet in soft white sand or in the waters of a cool mountain spring. Head out on two wheels to marvel at unspoiled landscapes. Join your kids in conquering medieval castles and lavish palaces. Immerse yourself in timeless local traditions. Indulge in Atlantic cuisine with a Mediterranean influence. Discover urban secrets and rural hideaways. Spot protected species at natural parks. Meander through vineyards, tasting reds, whites, greens and rosés. Unearth layer upon layer of absorbing history. Dance the night away and toast the rising sun.

This is Portugal.

TURN THE PAGE AND START PLANNING YOUR NEXT BEST TRIP →

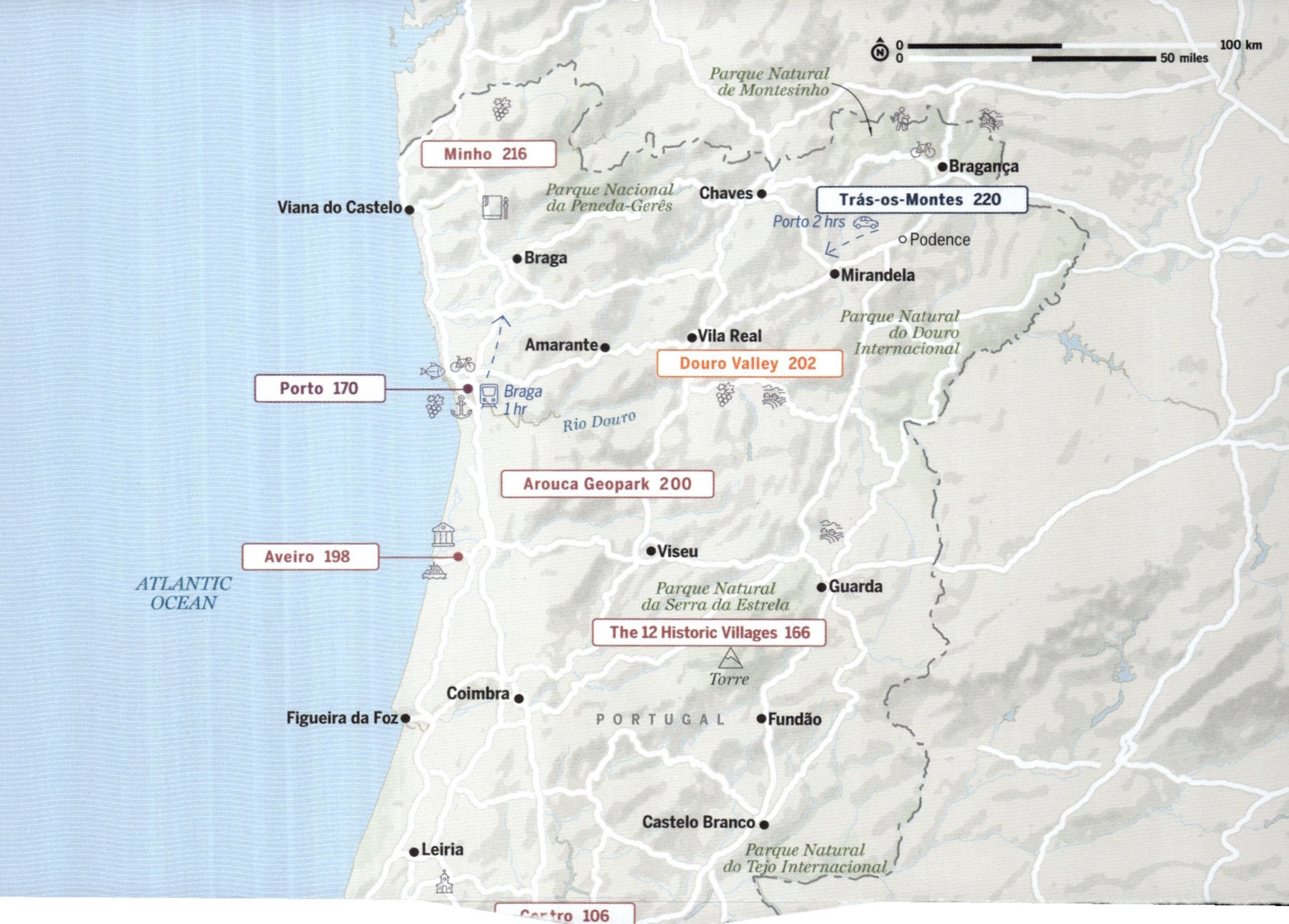

0 100 km
0 50 miles
Parque Natural de Montesinho
Minho 216
Bragança
Parque Nacional da Peneda-Gerês
Chaves
Trás-os-Montes 220
Viana do Castelo
Porto 2 hrs
Podence
Braga
Mirandela
Parque Natural do Douro Internacional
Amarante
Vila Real
Douro Valley 202
Porto 170
Braga 1 hr
Rio Douro
Arouca Geopark 200
Aveiro 198
Viseu
ATLANTIC OCEAN
Guarda
Parque Natural da Serra da Estrela
The 12 Historic Villages 166
Torre
Coimbra
Figueira da Foz
PORTUGAL
Fundão
Castelo Branco
Leiria
Parque Natural do Tejo Internacional

Praia da Marinha (p144)

Sandra Henriques

@s__henriques

Azores-born and Lisbon-based Sandra Henriques writes about travel, culture,and the people she meets in between for several publications. In 2021, she officially became a published author of horror short stories in Portuguese.

Marlene Marques

@marleneonthemove

Journalist and travel writer, Marlene specialises in nature and adventure travel and is co-founder of the Portuguese Travel Bloggers Association. When she's not travelling, you can always find this Lisbon-native exploring the beautiful Portuguese coastline.

Joana Taborda

@cityodes

Born-and-raised in Lisbon, Joana enjoys hopping on a train to little-known towns and drinking the local craft beer wherever she gets off. To escape winter, she spends her time between the capital and the semi-tropical island of Madeira.

Contents

MARCIN KRZYZAK/SHUTTERSTOCK ©

Ascensor da Bica (p77), Lisbon

FOODIE FACTS

Portugal boasts the highest fish consumption per capita in the EU.

Portugal has the highest rate of wine consumption per capita in the world.

ATLANTIC **CUISINE**

Portugal's location on the Atlantic Ocean, its proximity to the Mediterranean Sea and its colonial legacy have all contributed to its unique cuisine. In Portugal, bread and wine are a regular presence at every table, often serving as bookends for hearty dishes such as *bacalhau à lagareiro* (dried salt-cod baked in olive oil), a dish that brings together disparate waters and influences.

→ DRIED SALT-COD

Despite being fished thousands of miles from Portugal, in the North Atlantic, *bacalhau* (salt-cured cod) is one of the most emblematic Portuguese ingredients.

NATALIA MYLOVA/SHUTTERSTOCK ©

Left Grilled sardines **Right** Dried salt-cod **Below** Traditional Portuguese snacks

PORTION SIZES

At *tascas* (taverns) and other typical eateries, single portions are large enough to feed two. Order a *meia dose* (half-portion) if you don't have much of an appetite.

RIGHT: SEBASTIANA RAW/SHUTTERSTOCK ©

↑ COUVERT

In some restaurants, a spread of starters, known as *couvert,* is brought to your table, no questions asked. Before you start to nibble, note that it's *not* complimentary.

Best Food & Drink Experiences

- **Dip your toes in the local foodie scene by exploring Lisbon's traditional and contemporary restaurants (p54)**
- **Visit the Setúbal market, one of the country's best (p93)**
- **Try the cured ham from Iberian pigs, raised on acorns in the Alentejo (p128)**
- **Increase your tasting-note vocabulary at the Douro region's wineries (p208)**
- **Follow the trail of *tabernas* (simple restaurants) in the country's far north (p226)**

FAMILY **FUN**

The close to 300 days of sunshine are great excuses to spend time outdoors, letting the kids blow off steam while exploring local biodiversity. Historical and prehistorical sites make for great opportunities for fun learning. And the three days of Carnaval, celebrated all over the country in February/March, are perfect for children and adults alike to dress up as their favourite fictional characters.

Left Carnaval parade, Loulé (p157) **Right** Palácio Nacional da Pena (p89), Sintra **Below** Sand City sculptures

FAMILY PRICES

Some attractions offer special family prices. Family is used as a broad term for two adults and two children, or one adult and one child.

MUSEUM ACTIVITIES

Most activities for children at museums are held in Portuguese. If an activity catches your eye, ask beforehand if it's held in English.

CHILDREN'S FILMS

International films for kids under six are released in two versions: subtitled (VO – *versão original*) and dubbed (VP – *versão Portuguesa*).

Best Family Experiences

- **Explore medieval castles and luxurious palaces in the UNESCO World Heritage town of Sintra (p88)**
- **Sign up for horse-riding lessons in the Algarve with Albufeira Riding Centre (p149)**
- **Discover the pop-culture sand sculptures at Sand City Lagoa (p164)**
- **Go for a treetop walk or visit the farm animals at Porto's Parque de Serralves (p175)**
- **Earn your keep at an *agro-turismo* or farm stay in the Alentejo (p127)**

DRIVING FAST FACTS

Drive on the right-hand side of the road.

Most cars are manual.

The legal driving age is 18.

The top speed limit is 120km/h on major highways.

PEDAL TO **THE METAL**

Portugal is the ultimate road-trip destination. You can drive from north to south in around six hours, meaning minimal time behind the wheel, and more time for exploring on foot. Great roads that reach just about every corner of the country mean driving is a breeze here. And the views are consistently amazing.

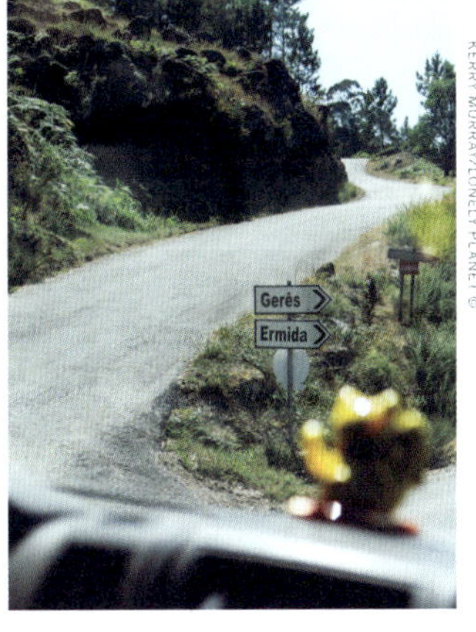

KERRY MURRAY/LONELY PLANET ©

Left Driving in the Parque Natural da Serra da Arrábida (p95) **Right** Road through the Parque Nacional da Peneda-Gerês (p218) **Below** Highway toll booths

RENTING A CAR

To rent a car in Portugal, you have to be 21 years or over and, for the major rental companies at least, have a credit or debit card.

LICENCE

An International Driving Permit (IDP) is not required when renting a car but it can be useful in the event of an accident or police stop.

RIGHT: MAURO RODRIGUES/SHUTTERSTOCK ©, LEFT: SOPOTNICK/SHUTTERSTOCK ©

↑ TOLLS

Many of the larger *autoestradas* (highways) in Portugal charge tolls.

Best Driving Experiences

- **Criss-cross the Minho's ever-green landscapes (p216)**
- **Buzz between churches, castles, vineyards and villages on the Rota da Terra Fria Trans-montana (p234)**
- **Ascend to hilltop villages dotted with castles in the Alentejo (p112)**
- **Make meals the destination while driving the Tabernas do Alto Tâmega (p226)**
- **Visit remote beaches along the Costa Vicentina (p134)**

HIT THE TRAILS

It doesn't matter if you're just getting started or your weathered boots are covered with the dust of a thousand hikes – in Portugal there is a trail for everyone. Explore the country's only national park, uncover cascades, or feel the salt on your skin as you hike the coast.

TOP: NEIRFY/GETTY IMAGES ©, BOTTOM: HANS SLEGERS/SHUTTERSTOCK ©

★ RESPONSIBLE HIKING

Particularly in biosphere reserves, natural parks or other protected areas, stay on the trails and respect local wildlife.

★ HUNTING SEASON

Mid-August to late February is hunting season. Look for the red and white *zona de caça* signs.

Best Hiking Experiences

- **Link the Algarve and the Alentejo via the trails of the Costa Vicentina (p134)**
- **Trek between mountains and dunes at Parque Natural da Serra da Arrábida (p95)**
- **Visit central Portugal's 12 historic villages via the 600km Grand Route (p166)**
- **Opt between the 14 trails that make up northern Portugal's Arouca Geopark (p200)**
- **Visit the country's sole national park, Peneda-Gerês (p218)**

Above left Parque da Pena, Sintra (p88) **Left** Hiking the Costa Vicentina (p135)

SADDLE UP & CYCLE

Pedal along the rugged coast or brave the hilly inland and uncover remote villages. Go solo or on a family adventure. Hop on your favourite two-wheeler and bike through Portugal any time of the year, exploring at your own pace or booking a guided tour with expert cyclists.

TOP: ENRIQUE DIAZ/7CERO/GETTY IMAGES © BOTTOM: UMOMOS/SHUTTERSTOCK ©

★ KNOW BEFORE YOU GO

Although the landscape is beautiful, hills, aggressive drivers and the lack of a hard shoulder are consistent challenges when cycling on Portugal's roads.

Best Cycling Experiences

- Hire a bike and ride the coast from Cascais to Praia do Guincho (p87)
- Cycle across the Algarve on the Via Algarviana (p149)
- Explore Portugal's northeast on the Rota da Terra Fria (p234)
- Go from city to country on the Ecopista de Évora (p119)
- Cross the Tagus River from Lisbon and cycle from Trafaria to São João da Caparica (p74)

ACCOMMODATION

Wild camping is not allowed, so plan your stays between different stages of a route. There are plenty of accommodation options along the way.

Above left Cyclist in the Algarve (p149) **Left** Cycling in Aveiro (p198)

FABULOUS **FESTIVITIES**

Pick any month in the calendar, and some place in Portugal is most likely commemorating something. From nationwide celebrations of public holidays to super-niche food and cultural festivals, any excuse is great to party. During the summer the season picks up speed, with festivals ranging from musical events with top line-ups to small-town fairs and fetes.

Left Decorations for the Festival Internacional de Chocolate (p97), Óbidos **Right** Festival F, Faro **Below** Craft stall, Paderne Medieval Festival

MÚSICA PIMBA

Small-town festivals aren't complete without *música pimba*. Made for dancing, regardless of personal preferences, songs are upbeat with saucy, corny and punny lyrics, full of innuendo.

MUSIC FESTIVALS

Dozens of music festivals crowd the Portuguese events calendar in the summer. Diversity reigns supreme, so pick according to favourite genre, location or travelling dates.

↑ LOCAL CRAFTS

In addition to sampling traditional food, smaller events outside major urban centres are a great opportunity to see and buy local crafts.

Best Festive Experiences

- ▶ **Visit Óbidos in the spring for the Festival Internacional de Chocolate (p97)**
- ▶ **Learn about the smuggling past of Alcoutim at Festival do Contrabando (p164)**
- ▶ **Dance to Celtic folk music in August at the Festival Intercéltico de Sendim in Trás-os-Montes (p236)**
- ▶ **Celebrate wine, wine and more wine at the Pombaline Festival (p214)**
- ▶ **Witness colourfully masked locals welcoming spring at the Carnaval de Podence (p236)**

STATE OF RULE

Portugal was a monarchy until 5 October 1910.

On 28 May 1926 a coup instated a conservative dictatorship (Estado Novo).

On 25 April 1974 a military coup defeated the dictatorship (Revolução dos Cravos).

PIECES OF **THE PAST**

Tucked between Spain and the Atlantic Ocean, rectangle-shaped Portugal has officially been a country since 1143, one of the oldest in the world. For eight centuries, and before that, a plethora of cultural influences swept the nation, creating a Portuguese identity that locals have trouble explaining. Portugal's history is complex and its past as a colonising country shaped a future that must be reinvented. Bear witness to all the layers.

SAIKO3P/SHUTTERSTOCK ©

Left Cromeleque dos Almendres (p119), Évora **Right** Mosteiro dos Jerónimos (p69), Lisbon **Below** Convento do Carmo (p69), Lisbon

→ COLONIAL PAST

Wounds are fresh and far from healed. But in recent years, there's been an attempt (albeit slow) to acknowledge Portugal's colonial past.

▶ Learn more on p70

AGE OF DISCOVERIES

Portrayed as a country of conquerors, in Portugal the so-called 'Age of Discoveries' is frequently used as the symbol of great feats.

RIGHT: KATVIC/SHUTTERSTOCK ©; LEFT: MRFOTOS/SHUTTERSTOCK ©

GREAT EARTHQUAKE

The Great Earthquake of 1755 not only shattered Lisbon but had a profound impact on Voltaire and other key thinkers during the Age of Enlightenment.

Best Historic Experiences

- ▶ Visit the marks, both seen and unseen, of the 1755 Great Earthquake in Lisbon (p69)
- ▶ Learn about Portugal's role in the trading of enslaved people at the Antigo Mercado de Escravos in Lagos (p164)
- ▶ Get in touch with the country's ancient past in the UNESCO city of Évora (p118)
- ▶ Explore preserved Iron Age settlements in Minho (p219)
- ▶ Stroll the streets of Porto's Ribeira, one of the city's oldest neighbourhoods (p184)

The minimum legal age to drink alcohol is 18 years.

Bars generally close at around 2am or 3am.

Nightclubs typically close at the crack of dawn, any time between 4am and 6am.

OUT ON THE TOWN

Nights are warm in the summer and tolerably cold in the winter. If that's not a good excuse to go out on the weekends, how about affordable drinks? The working Portuguese reserve all their partying energy for Friday and Saturday nights. The habit of post-work drinks has not settled in, but on weekends late dinners turn into early night caps that lead to dancing until dawn.

Left Evening street scene, Lisbon **Right** *Porto Tónico* (white port with tonic water and lemon; p189) **Below** *Santos populares* celebration, Lisbon

FRÁGIL'S LEGACY

Frágil, a bar that once existed in Bairro Alto, was partially responsible for the cultural and musical awakening of 1980s Lisbon after 40+ years of a conservative dictatorship.

ADRIENNE PITTS/LONELY PLANET ©

OUTDOOR DRINKING

Grabbing a drink at the bar and joining your friends outside is standard behaviour. Weather permitting, outdoor sitting areas fill up fast.

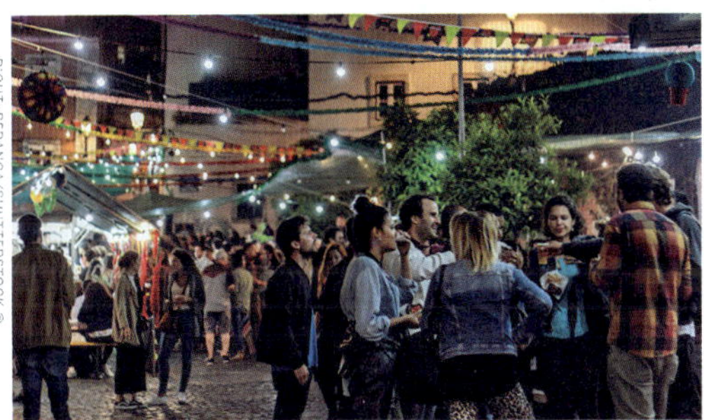

RIGHT: RFRANCA/SHUTTERSTOCK © LEFT: TRABANTOS/SHUTTERSTOCK ©

↑ SANTOS POPULARES

In June, during *santos populares* (street festivals paying homage to the popular saints Anthony, John and Peter), all etiquette rules go out the window. The streets of Porto and Lisbon are packed and people dance to live *música pimba*.

Best Nightlife Experiences

- **Watch the sunrise as you party til dawn at Lux-Frágil, one of Lisbon's top clubs (p58)**
- **Bar-hop in Porto's residential Ribeira neighbourhood by day and party by night (p194)**
- **Toast the sunset and party all night on Albufeira's bar-clad strip (p159)**
- **Paint the town pink at Lisbon's revitalised and reinvented Cais do Sodré area (p60)**

WINE PARTICULARS

The Douro and the Alentejo are Portugal's largest wine-producing regions.

France, the US and the UK are the largest importers of Portuguese wine.

Vinho Verde is a region, not the name of a grape or a blend.

FROM GRAPE **TO GLASS**

Although the Douro Valley and Alentejo get most of the attention, Portugal has 14 different wine regions and they cover all areas of the country. More than a drink, wine is practically a basic need and an intricate part of locals' diet. With some of the oldest vineyards on earth, wine has played a key role in the country's cultural identity since Roman times.

Left Douro Valley vineyards
Right Wine store, Lisbon
Below Wine with a view

→ REASONABLE PRICES

You can buy decent wines at supermarkets, at reasonable prices, and from reputed wine producers. Reserve boxed wine for seasoning food and making sangria.

GREG ELMS/LONELY PLANET ©

WINE QUALITY

Table wine is *vinho de mesa* (basic and cheaper), then up a notch is *vinho regional,* and DOC are the wines under strict quality control.

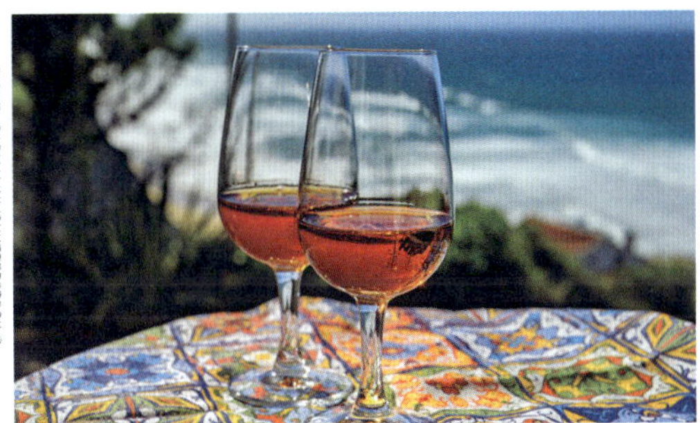

RIGHT: BARMALINI/SHUTTERSTOCK © LEFT: HERMITIS/SHUTTERSTOCK ©

WINE VARIETY

Follow your tastebuds to find the wine that pairs perfectly with you. You might arrive in Portugal loving reds and leave ditching them for crisp young whites.

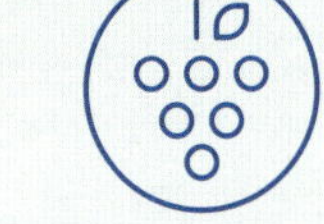

Best Wine Experiences

- **Explore the mighty and lush Douro Valley, for the wine and cultural experiences (p210)**
- **Taste Setúbal's sweet and fruity Moscatel (p94)**
- **Relax at a yoga class with wine at Alentejo's Adega Mayor (p131)**
- **Sign up for a tasting of the city's famous port wine in Porto (p190)**
- **Lunch on a family vineyard in the shade of a thousand-year-old tree in the Algarve's Morgado do Quintão (p165)**

SURF'S UP

Half of Portugal's territory is coast, with sprawling beaches ranging from the cold and tumultuous north to the balmy and laid-back south. Not surprising given its geography, one of the country's greatest pulls is its waves. Nazaré is home to the largest waves ever surfed, while dozens of beaches along the coast function as open-air surf schools for beginners. In short, the country accommodates surfers of every level.

Left Surfer, Praia do Norte, Nazaré (p41) **Right** Praia do Nazaré **Below** Beach near Ericeira (p41)

WHEN TO SURF

Spring and autumn tend to be the best seasons for surfing. Waves at this time range from 2m to 4.5m high.

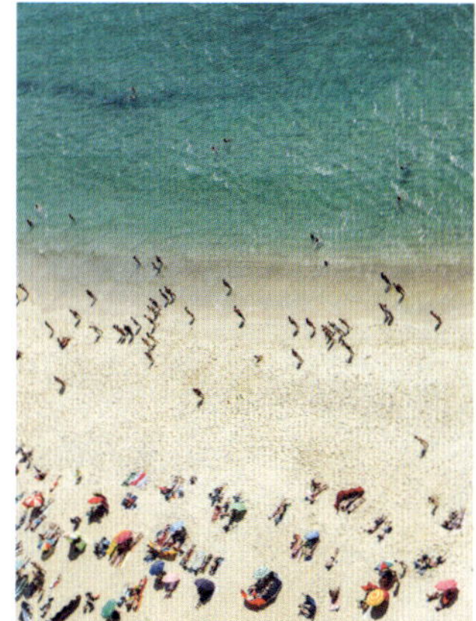

DAVID LOPES/GETTY IMAGES ©

WHAT TO TAKE

The water temperature in Portugal is colder than most other southern European countries, and you'll probably want a wetsuit, even in summer.

RIGHT: KERRY MURRAY/LONELY PLANET ©; LEFT: HOMYDESIGN/SHUTTERSTOCK ©

TUITION

Surf camps typically offer weekly packages that include simple accommodation (dorms, bungalows, camping), meals and transport to the beach.

Best Surfing Spots

- **Hop on the commuter train from Lisbon and surf at Carcavelos (p87)**
- **Head to L-Point in Porto Covo (p124) for the best fun on the waves.**
- **Surf the wild, near-deserted beaches lining the Costa Vicentina (p134)**
- **Ditch Porto and hit the surf at Praia de Matosinhos (p196)**
- **Ride the Atlantic waves at the Algarve's Praia de Odeceixe (p145)**

Santos Populares

During June, festivities sprout all over the country to honour the popular saints *(santos populares)* Anthony, John and Peter.

↙ Music Festivals

Dozens of events with catchy line-ups compete for attention. NOS Alive is among the most popular festivals in Europe.

📍 Lisbon

▸ nosalive.com

School's out in July and August, which means families ditch the cities for stints in the countryside or at the beach.

Day of Portugal

Portugal celebrates its national holiday on 10 June. Expect some places and attractions to be closed.

JUNE

Average daytime max: 25°C
Days of rainfall: 2 (Lisbon)

JULY

Portugal in SUMMER

↓ Arraial Lisboa Pride

The largest LGBTIQ+ event in Portugal is a two-week-long celebration in Lisbon that ends with a parade down Avenida da Liberdade.

Lisbon

▸ ilga-portugal.pt/lisboapride

With late sunsets, enjoy the outdoors as much as possible, be it exploring a park or lounging at an *esplanada* (open-air terrace).

↑ Olhão Seafood Festival

Seafood lovers should not miss this grand culinary fest. Highlights include regional specialities like chargrilled fish, *caldeirada* (fish stew) and *cataplana* (seafood stew).

Olhão, p152

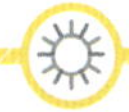

AUGUST

Average daytime max: 28°C
Days of rainfall: 0

Average daytime max: 28°C
Days of rainfall: 1

Peak Season

Demand for accommodation peaks during summer. Book transfers, tours and overnight adventures in advance.

Packing Notes

Pack a hat and sunscreen as the average UV index soars up to 10.

The school year restarts in mid-September. Expect busier cities and traffic.

Republic Day

On 5 October, Portugal celebrates the start of the Republican regime. Several events take place on this national holiday.

End of the Beach Season

Beach season ends on 15 September for most of Portugal, but hot days linger. Most beaches go unguarded after this date.

↖ Grape Harvesting Season

Between August and early October wine regions in Portugal are bustling with harvesting activity. It's a great time to tour wineries.

SEPTEMBER

Average daytime max: 26°C
Days of rainfall: 3 (Lisbon)

OCTOBER

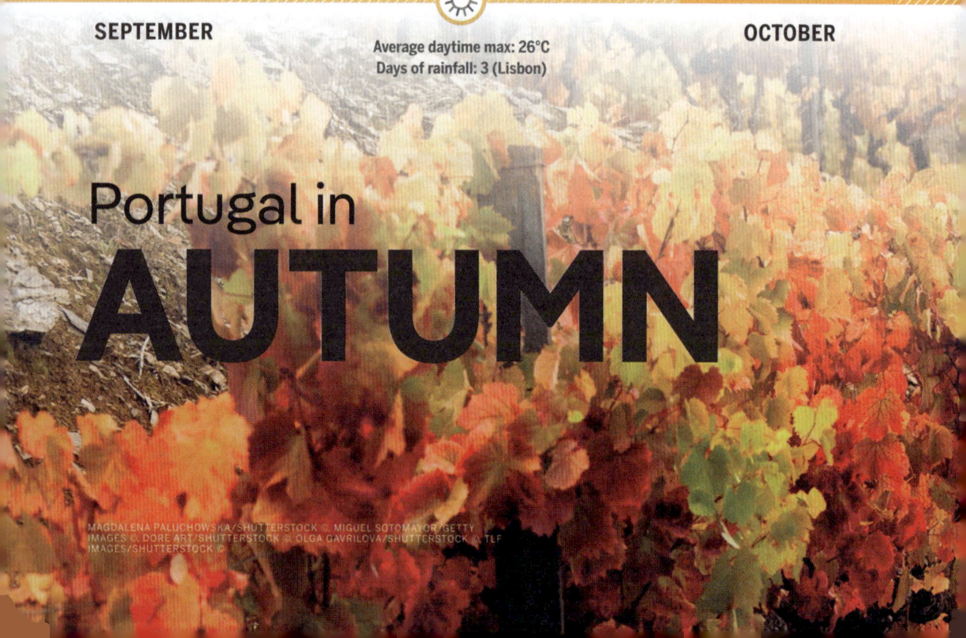

Portugal in AUTUMN

October is the start of low season. With fewer crowds and lower temperatures, it can be an ideal time to visit.

Although the north and the west coast can be cold and wet in November, the south and the Alentejo still get plenty of sunshine. Expect excellent prices and thin crowds.

↗ All Saints Day

1 November is a Catholic national holiday celebrating All Saints.

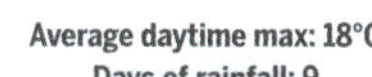

NOVEMBER

Average daytime max: 23°C
Days of rainfall: 8

Average daytime max: 18°C
Days of rainfall: 9

Packing Notes

Pack light options and warmer clothes to layer up, plus easy-to-carry rain gear for occasional showers.

↓ Holiday Season

Most places close on Christmas Day (25 December) and New Year's Day (1 January). Streets light up with decorations; *pastelarias* (pastry and cake shops) are fully stocked.

↓ Big-Wave Season

Surfers head to the beaches on the west this time of year for a chance to ride a giant wave.

National Holidays

1 and 8 December are national holidays, but most businesses are open because of holiday season.

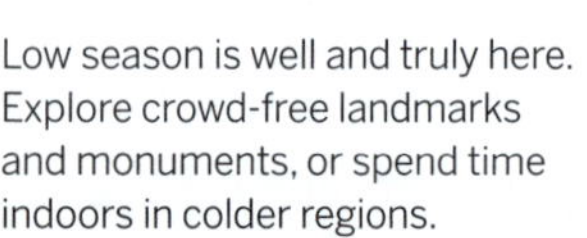

Low season is well and truly here. Explore crowd-free landmarks and monuments, or spend time indoors in colder regions.

DECEMBER

Average daytime max: 15°C
Days of rainfall: 10 (Lisbon)

JANUARY

Portugal in WINTER

Fantasporto

This world-renowned two-week international festival celebrates fantasy, horror and just plain weird films.

Porto

▸ fantasporto.com

↗ Carnaval

From traditional old pagan rituals to Brazil-inspired colourful parades, for three days (Sunday to Shrove Tuesday) most Portuguese celebrate Carnaval.

Podence, p225

Average daytime max: 15°C
Days of rainfall: 10

FEBRUARY

Average daytime max: 16°C
Days of rainfall: 8

→ Winter flurries

Occasional snowfall in Trás-os-Montes, close to the Spanish border.

Packing Notes

Pack warm, waterproof clothes and footwear. Expect snow in higher places.

↘ Nature Awakes

Spring is a great time to explore the outdoors as flowers bloom and mating season starts for most wildlife species.

← Easter Holidays

Schools close for two weeks during Easter. Some families take off from urban centres for a long-weekend getaway.

It's not yet high season, but tourists from neighbouring Spain often spend the long weekend in Portugal during Easter holidays.

MARCH

Average daytime max: 18°C
Days of rainfall: 6 (Lisbon)

APRIL

Portugal in SPRING

↘ 25 April

Liberty Day is one of the most important and widely celebrated national holidays. On this day in 1974 a military coup ended the dictatorship.

Festival Internacional de Chocolate

Celebrate the sweet temptation of the cacao bean with culinary presentations by top chocolate makers and hands-on cooking activities for kids.

Óbidos, p97

▸ festivalchocolate.cm-obidos.pt

MAY

Average daytime max: 20°C
Days of rainfall: 7

Average daytime max: 22°C
Days of rainfall: 5

← Fátima Romarias

Hundreds of thousands make the pilgrimage to Fátima to commemorate the apparitions of the Virgin that occurred on 13 May 1917.

Fátima, p106

Packing Notes

Light clothes for warm afternoons; warm clothes for chilly mornings and evenings.

LISBON
Trip Builder

TAKE YOUR PICK OF MUST-SEES AND HIDDEN GEMS

Lisbon has emerged as one of Europe's coolest cities – an achingly beautiful metropolis that combines the charm and laid-back vibe of a small town with the cosmopolitan energy of a major hub.

Trip Notes

How long Allow a week

Getting around Public transport is pretty efficient, combining a decent metro with a network of buses and picturesque tramways. The metro is most useful when venturing further afield (to the airport, for example).

Tips If you're staying within the city centre, the most efficient way to get around is on foot, provided you have good walking shoes. Lisbon's trademark mosaic sidewalks can be treacherously slippery.

Chiado
In this upscale area, you'll find charming squares and buildings that have retained their Art Nouveau facades.
½ day

Alcântara
Alcântara has used rust and iron to its advantage, turning a bridge and an old factory into tourist attractions.
½ hour from Lisbon

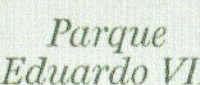

Bairro Alto

Narrow streets, cosy restaurants and brash bars shape this nightlife area.

½ day

Baixa

Shaped by the Great Earthquake of 1755, Baixa's perfectly laid-out streets and squares are a testament to the Marquês de Pombal's vision.

½ day

Graça

This graceful hilltop 'hood is home to tile-fronted 19th-century villas that accommodated a growing population of factory workers.

½ day

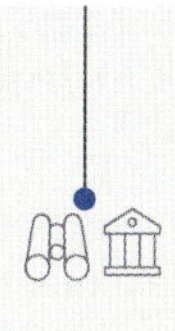

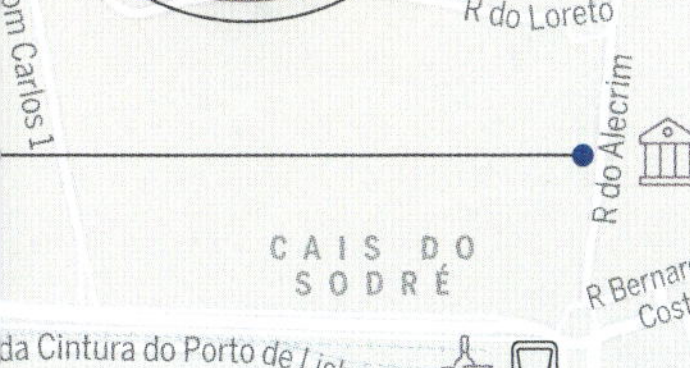

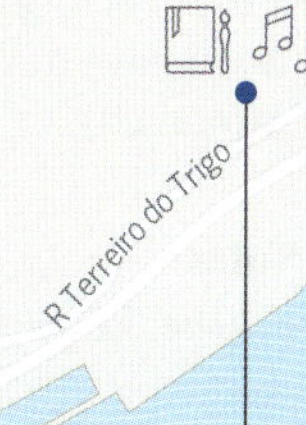

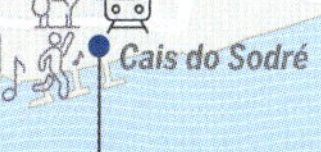

Alfama

Lisbon's oldest neighbourhood is the spiritual home of fado and has a Moorish-era layout.

½ day

Praça do Comércio

Extending along the Tagus RIver, this monumental plaza feels like the gateway to the city.

½ day

Cais do Sodré

This raucous riverside strip is Lisbon's unofficial entertainment zone, home to a string of bars and clubs that stay up late.

½ day

BEYOND LISBON
Trip Builder

TAKE YOUR PICK OF MUST-SEES AND HIDDEN GEMS

Be captivated by fine sandy beaches, venture along the Tejo riverbanks, enjoy the local wine and discover world heritage. For a taste of the best that Portugal has to offer, you don't even have to venture far from the capital city.

Trip Notes

Hubs Lisbon, Sintra, Setúbal

How long Allow 7 days

Getting around There is frequent public transport such as bus or train to take you to the main destinations. If you want greater flexibility, rent a car so you can stop along the way.

Tips Avoid leaving or entering Lisbon at rush hour as you may get stuck in traffic. In high season, seaside destinations and major monuments fill up with visitors, so go early.

Colares

Visit the incredible beaches of Ursa and Adraga and stop at Cabo da Roca, the westernmost tip of continental Europe. For this trip, you will need a car.

1 day

Parque Natural de Sintra-Cascais

Praia da Adraga

Praia Ursa

Cabo da Roca

Sintra

Praia do Guincho

Cascais

Atlantic Ocean

Cascais

Enjoy a round of golf overlooking the Atlantic, and then explore the town's museums and restaurants. Cycle or walk to Praia do Guincho along the wooden walkways that cross the protected sand dunes.

1–2 days

ESTREMADURA

Vila Franca de Xira

Discover contrasting landscapes in the Reserva Natural do Estuário do Tejo and go birdwatching in one of Portugal's most important wetlands.

1 day

Tapada Nacional de Mafra

Mafra

Mafra

Visit the Palácio Nacional de Mafra, a UNESCO World Heritage Site. Then go for a walk in the Tapada Nacional de Mafra and see the deer.

1–2 days

Vila Franca de Xira

Río Tejo

Alverca do Ribatejo

Rio Sorraia

Reserva Natural do Estuário do Tejo

Rio Tejo

LISBON

Palmela

Hop between eight viewpoints in the town of Palmela and enjoy a glass of the famous regional wine.

2 days

Rio Tejo

Almada

Setúbal Peninsula

Costa da Caparica

Spread your towel or have a surf session on dozens of beaches that stretch for 13km. See the gorgeous view from the top of the Arriba Fóssil.

1 day

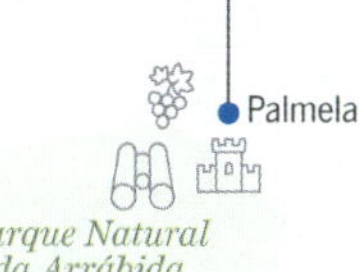

Palmela

Parque Natural da Arrábida

0 — 20 km
0 — 10 miles

THE ALGARVE
Trip Builder

TAKE YOUR PICK OF MUST-SEES AND HIDDEN GEMS

Cliff-flanked coves, secluded sea caves and islands of golden sands decorate the coast – inviting surfers, water-sports fanatics and beachcombers. Inland, whitewashed villages and mountainous hiking trails provide a peaceful retreat.

Trip Notes

Hubs Faro, Albufeira, Lagos

How long Allow 10 days

Getting around Hiring a car will give access to remote bays and inland villages. Trains and buses link main towns and beaches; boat trips are in abundance from tourist hubs.

Tips All beaches in the Algarve are public. Early risers will enjoy peaceful sands and calmer waters, though a quieter stretch is often only a short walk away.

São Teotónio

Costa Vicentina & Sagres
Road trip, or hike, along the striking and lesser-visited west coast, exploring vast sands, epic surf and the dramatic cliffs of Cabo de São Vicente, mainland Portugal's most southwesterly point.
2 days

Serra do Monchiqu

Fóia

Casais

Sagres

Cabo de São Vicente

Lagos

Lagos
Kayak through imposing sandstone towers at Ponta da Piedade before kicking back in traditional cafes and sipping cocktails in lively bars.
1 day

Atlantic Ocean

0 — 20 km
0 — 10 miles

Monchique

Trek the verdant trails in Serra de Monchique, reaching Fóia, the region's highest point. Reward yourself with relaxation at the thermal spa town of Caldas de Monchique.

1 day

Faro

Stroll through the historic Cidade Velha (old town) of the Algarve's capital, wine and dine with marina views, and detour to Estoi to visit the Roman ruins of Milreu.

1 day

Loulé

Discover castle walls and craft workshops in Loulé town, before biking or hiking the Algarve's interior, exploring traditional villages and the Queda do Vigário waterfall.

1 day

Tavira

Explore Tavira, one of the Algarve's most charming towns, home to a beautiful beach island and salt pans with seasonal flamingo sightings.

1 day

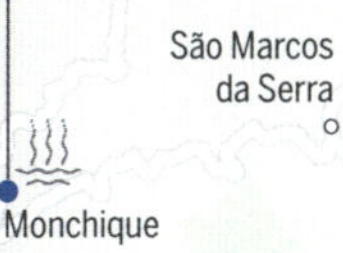

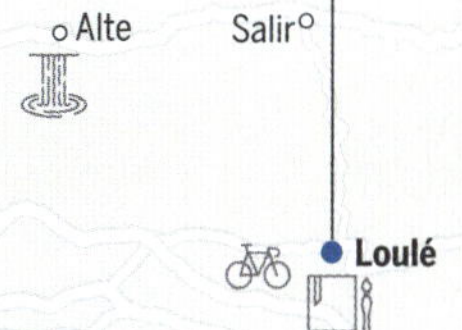

Carvoeiro to Albufeira

Beach-hop between idyllic coves and sea caves along this rugged stretch of coast, where water sports and boat trips to the poster-child Benagil Cave are easily accessible.

2 days

Olhão & Parque Natural da Ria Formosa

Pick up fresh seafood at Mercados de Olhão, take a ferry to serene islands in the Parque Natural da Ria Formosa, and admire birdlife among the dunes.

1 day

PORTO & THE NORTH
Trip Builder

TAKE YOUR PICK OF MUST-SEES AND HIDDEN GEMS

From the medieval to the modern, discover the diverse visual, cultural and gastronomic tapestry that is the north of Portugal. Some of Portugal's oldest villages, most closely held traditions and least touristed spots await you here.

Trip Notes

Hubs Porto, Peso da Régua, Valença, Guimarães

How long Allow 14 days

Getting around Hire a car to be spontaneous and let the spirit of adventure take you. Ease into the driving and take in the scenery by travelling counter-clockwise, leaving the bigger towns for the second week.

Tips In summer, save Peneda-Gerês for weekdays to avoid the weekend warriors. Forgo the expensive toll roads and take the leisurely and free national roads.

Valença
Use this walled border town as a base for exploring the popular pilgrim stop of Ponte de Lima and other lively towns along the border with Galicia.
2 days

Viana do Castelo
Take in the spectacular view from the mountaintop site of Santuário de Santa Luzia, then head to the beaches of the Costa Verde.
1 day

Porto
Explore Portugal's charming second city and get lost on purpose. Known as the gateway to the north, its steep historic centre will require your comfiest shoes.
3 days

SPAIN
Valença
ATLANTIC OCEAN
Ponte da Barca
PORTUGAL
Viana do Castelo
Braga
Póvoa de Varzim
Vila Nova de Famalicão
Villa do Conde
Porto
Aveiro

Parque Nacional da Peneda-Gerês
Hike Portugal's only national park, home to wild horses and two impressive shrines (Senhora da Peneda and São Bento da Porta Aberta).
2 days
0 50 km
0 25 miles
N
SPAIN
Montalegre
Parque Nacional da Peneda-Gerês
Chaves
Trás-os-Montes
Ramble the rugged landscapes and ruins of settlements, observing a disappearing way of life in this region colloquially referred to as 'behind the mountains'.
2 days
Guimarães
Stay in the birthplace of Portugal, visit the castle and the historic quarter before making a side jaunt to Braga, including Bom Jesus do Monte.
2 days
PORTUGAL
Mirandela
Guimarães
Parque Natural do Alvão
Valqueiro
Rio Tua
Vila Real
Amarante
Tua
Penafiel
Peso da Régua
Parque Natural do Douro Internacional
Rio Douro
SPAIN
Douro Valley
Unwind at the estates of the wine region while brushing up on your oenology, and tap into your inner archaeologist at the prehistoric sites of Parque Côa.
2 days

ALONG THE COAST
Trip Builder

TAKE YOUR PICK OF MUST-SEES AND HIDDEN GEMS

Fishing and shellfish-gathering traditions are in their histories, but these seaside towns are increasingly known for their great waves. Here, the seafood is just-off-the-boat fresh, the cliffs are rugged and wild, and the waves are magnificently challenging.

Trip Notes

Hubs Lisbon, Caldas da Rainha, Leiria

How long Allow 5 days

Getting around Rent a car and explore the coastal area at your own pace. If you decide to use public transport, be aware that you will probably have to make several transfers before you reach your destination.

Tips Opt for the roads along the coastline. It will certainly take longer, but the scenery is more pleasant, and you will save on highway tolls.

Atlantic Ocean

Foz do Arelho
Explore the wooden walkways that run along the cliffs of Foz do Arelho. Stand-up paddle-board or kayak in the calm waters of the Lagoa de Óbidos.
1 day

Reserva Natural das Berlenga

Santa Cruz
Walk along this extensive sandy beach and marvel at the cliffs of Ponta da Vigia and the Penedo do Guincho.
½ day

Pombal

São Pedro de Moel

Visit the peaceful seaside town, stroll through the Mata Nacional de Leiria, and explore the beaches that extend all the way to Nazaré.

1 day

Pinhal de Leiria

São Pedro de Moel

Leiria

Nazaré

Head to Avenida do Mar to see the traditional fish-drying stands. Visit the Santuário de Nossa Senhora da Nazaré and go to the Forte São Miguel Arcanjo to see Nazaré's famous giant waves.

1 day

Nazaré

Foz do Arelho

Caldas da Rainha

Parque Natural das Serras de Aire e Candeeiros

Lagoa de Óbidos

Peniche

If you want to learn to surf, you are in the right place. Travel along the cliffs to Farol do Cabo Carvoeiro, visit the old fortress, or take the boat to the Berlengas.

1–2 days

Peniche

RIBATEJO

Serra de Montejunto

Santa Cruz

Torres Vedras

ESTREMADURA

Ericeira

Try out your surfing skills in the World Surfing Reserve, the first in Europe. Go for a walk in the picturesque village and sample the fresh fish or seafood in one of the many local restaurants.

1–2 days

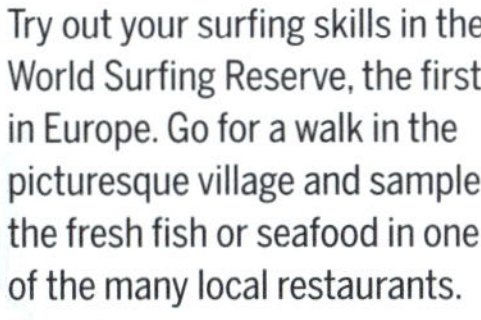

Ericeira

Parque Natural de Sintra-Cascais

Rio Tejo

LISBON

0 — 40 km

0 — 20 miles

THE ALENTEJO Trip Builder

TAKE YOUR PICK OF MUST-SEES AND HIDDEN GEMS

Oak trees lost in golden prairies come to mind when you speak of the Alentejo, Portugal's largest region. But this is also a land of hilltop castles, hidden beaches, fruitful vineyards and artisans creating beautiful tapestries and colourful ceramics.

Trip Notes

Hubs Évora, Beja, Elvas, Sines

How long Allow 10 days

Getting around Trains and buses connect Lisbon with the Alentejo's major cities, but hiring a car will get you much further at your own pace; tours are also an option.

Tips Roads are busy in summer, as people head to the Algarve, but when exiting to the Alentejo, traffic fades. If hiking, bring plenty of water: it's not always easy to find shade.

Arraiolos
Admire the hand-woven rugs that fill the streets and visit the circular castle on the outskirts.
½ day

Évora
Explore Neolithic sites, Roman ruins and Gothic churches in this UNESCO World Heritage city.
1 day

Porto Covo
Put your surfing skills to the test and sample seafood platters in this charming beach town. It's also the perfect starting point for hiking the Rota Vicentina, one of Europe's best coastal trails.
1–2 days

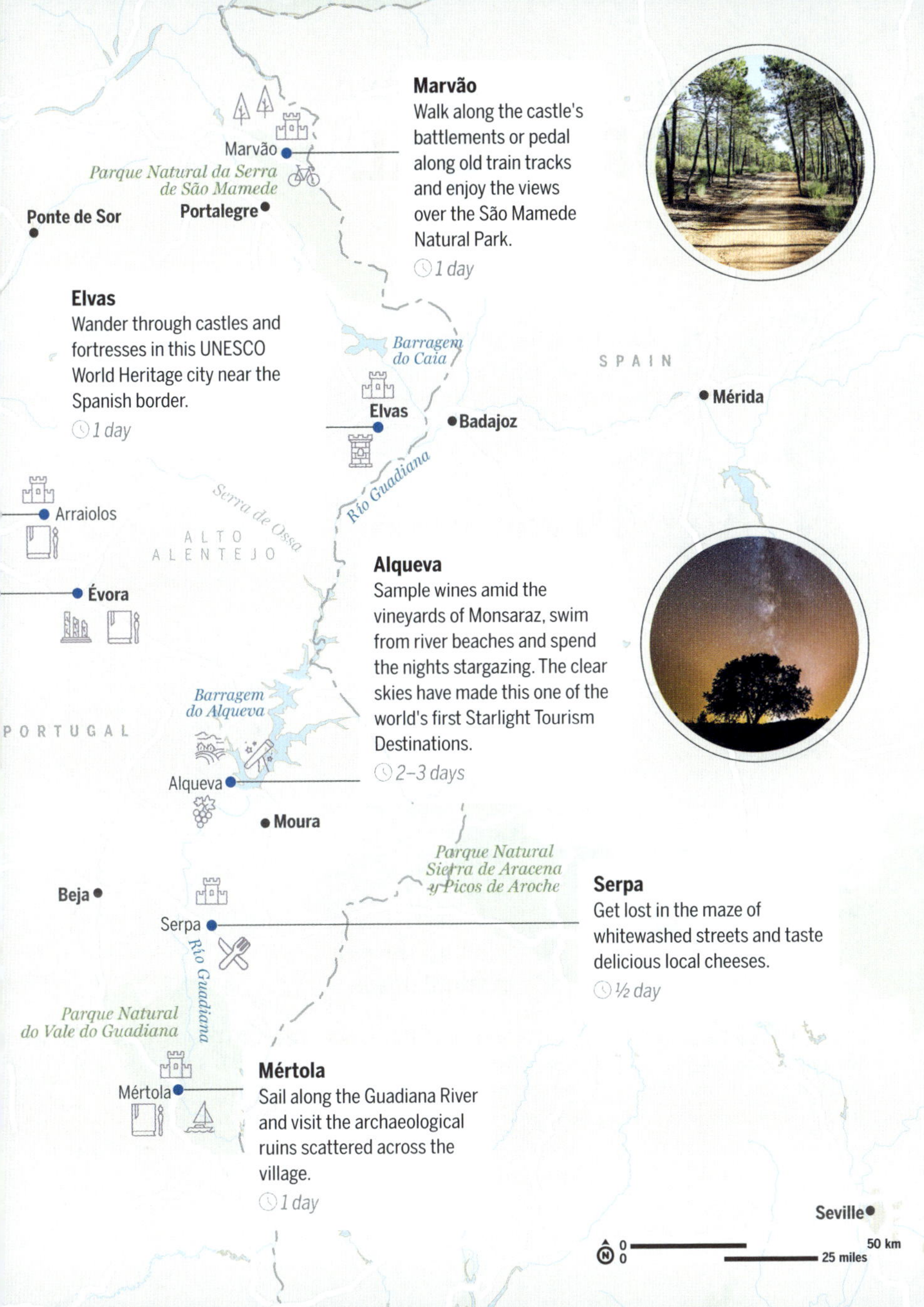

Marvão
Walk along the castle's battlements or pedal along old train tracks and enjoy the views over the São Mamede Natural Park.
1 day
Marvão
Parque Natural da Serra de São Mamede
Ponte de Sor
Portalegre
Elvas
Wander through castles and fortresses in this UNESCO World Heritage city near the Spanish border.
1 day
Barragem do Caia
SPAIN
Mérida
Elvas
Badajoz
Río Guadiana
Serra de Ossa
Arraiolos
ALTO ALENTEJO
Alqueva
Sample wines amid the vineyards of Monsaraz, swim from river beaches and spend the nights stargazing. The clear skies have made this one of the world's first Starlight Tourism Destinations.
2–3 days
Évora
Barragem do Alqueva
PORTUGAL
Alqueva
Moura
Parque Natural Sierra de Aracena y Picos de Aroche
Serpa
Get lost in the maze of whitewashed streets and taste delicious local cheeses.
½ day
Beja
Serpa
Río Guadiana
Parque Natural do Vale do Guadiana
Mértola
Sail along the Guadiana River and visit the archaeological ruins scattered across the village.
1 day
Mértola
Seville
0 50 km
0 25 miles

7 Things to Know About PORTUGAL

INSIDER TIPS TO HIT THE GROUND RUNNING

1 Embrace the detours

At first sight, Portugal might seem like a country easy to fully explore in just a few weeks. But no matter how well you plan the time you'll spend on the ground, the local historical and cultural richness, intriguing and mixed cuisine, and the people you meet will most likely have you chasing an off-the-map adventure. Go with the flow, Portuguese-style, and embrace the detours.

2 Portuguese is not Spanish

Most Portuguese, especially younger people, are fairly fluent in one foreign language. Near the border, locals will most likely speak fluent Spanish. That said, even though no one will call you out on the faux pas, don't think both languages sound the same or that everyone in the country speaks both.

▸ Discover the basics of Portuguese on p252

3 Sit for meals

Grabbing a quick bite is rare and most likely a product of an unexpected emergency. Mealtime is normally a sit-down experience at the table, whether you're lunching solo or meeting friends for dinner.

4 Soak up the sun in small doses

On average, Portugal has around 300 days of sunshine a year, so there's no need to get it all under your skin in one go.

▸ See more about the seasons on p24

5 A young democracy

Portugal's democracy is barely 50 years old. Some wounds remain very exposed still: the country's colonial past; five decades of an ultra-conservative dictatorship; the political prisoners who faced torture and persecution. As Portugal reckons with its past, there is an effort now to open up to much-needed, albeit difficult, conversations. The process is ongoing, but slow.

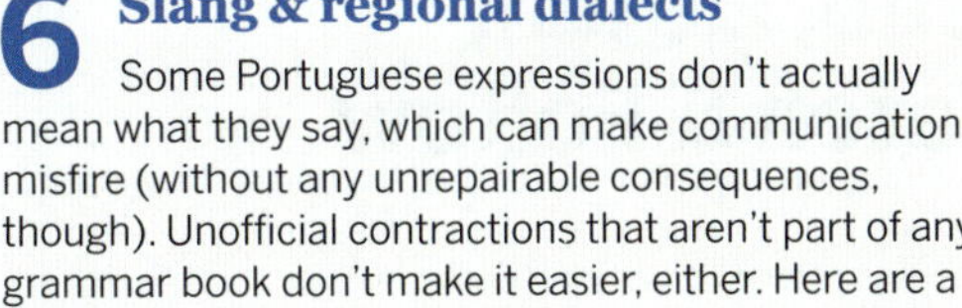

6 Slang & regional dialects

Some Portuguese expressions don't actually mean what they say, which can make communication misfire (without any unrepairable consequences, though). Unofficial contractions that aren't part of any grammar book don't make it easier, either. Here are a few examples.

tudo bem? – more of an end-all phrase than an actual expression of concern from the person asking how you are

então – a flexible word that changes meaning at each inflection. It can be a short form of a concerned question or a replacement for 'hello' *(então?)*, a polite 'watch it' *(então!)*, or a pause someone makes before starting a lengthy explanation *(então...)*

t'fona-me – a super-contracted short form for *telefona-me* (call me), mainly used in the Greater Lisbon area

In addition, regional dialects make the language even more colourful (and challenging), like the penchant for Northerners to replace the v with b (*vaca*, Portuguese for cow, becomes *baca*, for example).

7 Kissing strangers

The Portuguese are friendly and welcoming and, in a pre-Covid-19 world, reserved handshakes for professional encounters. Women meeting friends or strangers being introduced to someone for the first time typically greet each other with a quick kiss on each cheek. Men usually shake hands, sometimes elaborately. Hugging is generally reserved for more intimate relationships.

Read, Listen, Watch & Follow

READ

The Book of Disquiet (Fernando Pessoa/Bernardo Soares; 1982) Unedited pieces of text published posthumously.

A Short Book on the Great Earthquake (Rui Tavares; 2020) The events that shook Lisbon on 1 November 1755.

Journey to Portugal (José Saramago; 1990) Tales of cultural discovery while travelling through Portugal.

Escape Goat (2020) A serial novel written by 46 contemporary Portuguese authors during the Covid-19 pandemic.

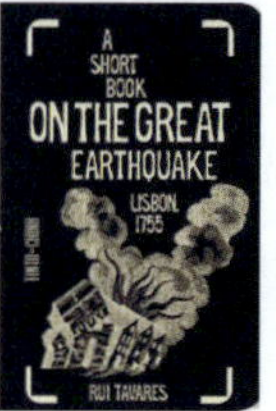

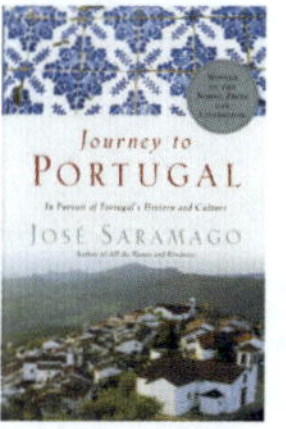

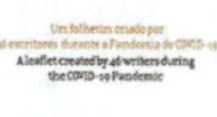

LISTEN

Excuse Me (Salvador Sobral; 2016) Debut album of the jazz and soul singer who won the Eurovision Song Contest in 2017.

Encore (Capicua; 2021) Porto-based Portuguese rapper and hip-hop musician launched this EP featuring her last concerts performed in 2020 before the Covid-19 lockdown.

Mariza Canta Amália (Mariza; 2020) Fado singer Mariza (pictured right) pays tribute to diva Amália Rodrigues with a record of her best songs.

Wolfheart (Moonspell; 1995) The debut album that propelled the gothic metal band into fame, both nationally and internationally.

TIM J GRAY/SHUTTERSTOCK ©

Lisboa Mulata (Dead Combo; 2011) The band's instrumental rock-and-blues-fusion fourth album pays tribute to Lisbon's multicultural diversity.

WATCH

Belarmino (Fernando Lopes; 1964) This docufiction on former boxer Belarmino signals the birth of Cinema Novo in Portugal.

Lisbon Story (Wim Wenders; 1994; pictured right) Drama/musical shot in Lisbon, featuring former Madredeus' lead singer Teresa Salgueiro.

Vitalina Varela (2019) Drama feature film directed by Pedro Costa (pictured left) in which Cape Verdean Vitalina Varela plays a fictionalised version of herself.

Os Filhos do Rock (Pedro Varela; 2013) TV show inspired by Portugal's 1980s rock-music generation.

Capitães de Abril (Maria de Medeiros; 2000) Story of how the peaceful military coup overthrew the dictatorship in 1974.

TOP: UNITED ARCHIVES/GETTY IMAGES © BOTTOM: UNIMEDIA/SHUTTERSTOCK ©

FOLLOW

tur4all.pt
Accessible tourism resources, including news, tips and tour companies.

portugalmanual.com
Network of Portuguese contemporary artisans and entrepreneurs.

portuguesetrails.com
All the information on hiking and cycling trails.

nazarewaves.com
Tune in here for big wave updates.

Portugal Farm Experiences

portugalfarm experience.com
Tours and activities at working farms.

LISBON
CHILL | CHARMING | OLD SCHOOL

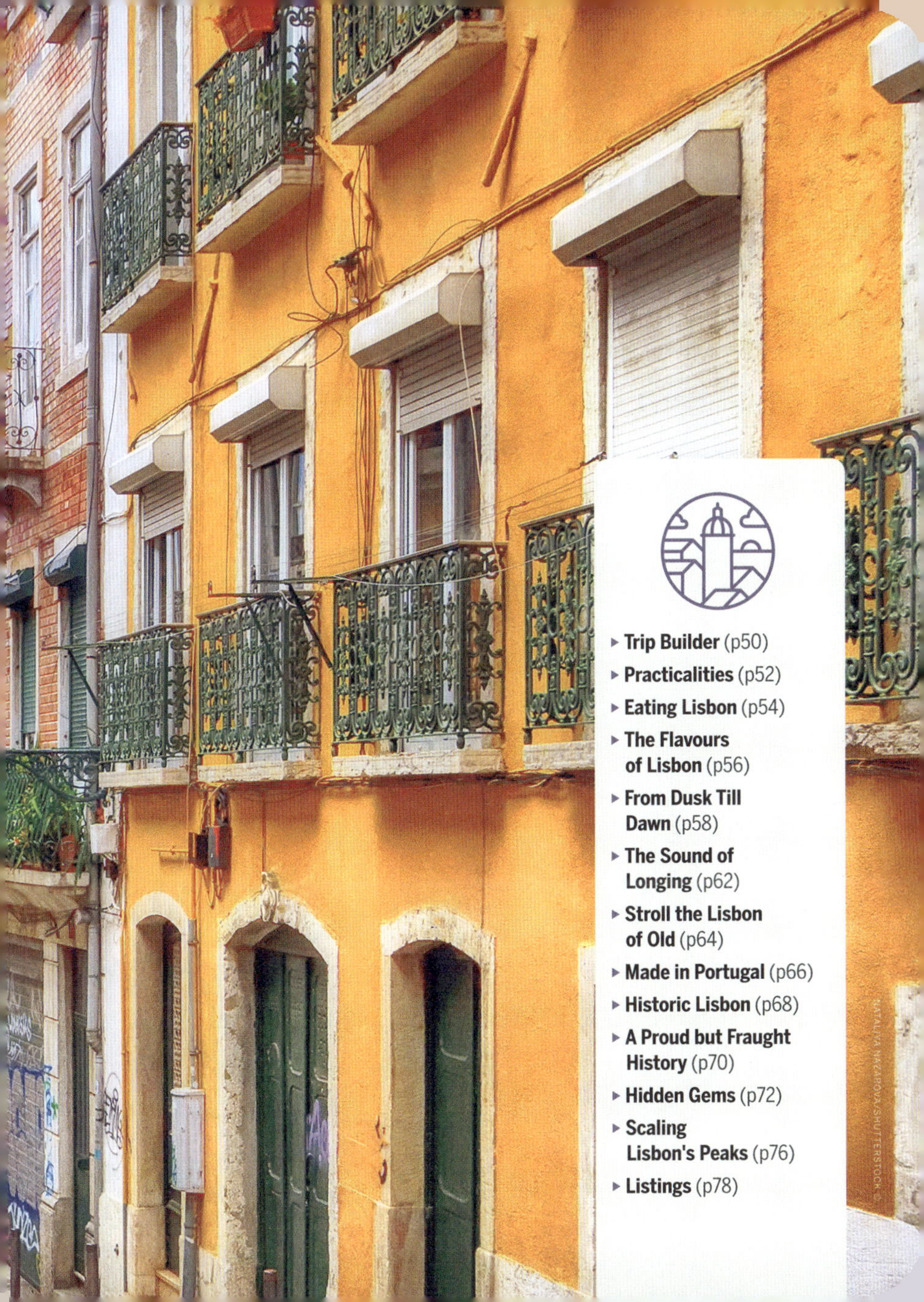

NATALIYA NAZAROVA/SHUTTERSTOCK ©

LISBON
Trip Builder

In one of Europe's coolest metropolises, soak up the pastel cityscape over a glass of wine at a hill-top park, examine the city's remarkable but fraught history, and delve into a nightlife scene that fuses Brazilian and African beats along with homegrown musical traditions.

R Ramalho Ortigão

R São Felipe Nery

Av Pedro Alvares Cabral

Dip into the flavours of Lisbon at **Pica-Pau** (p78)
2 hours

Taste Portuguese wines at **Black Sheep** (p80)
2 hours

Av Infante Santo

LAPA

Acesso a Ponte

Alcântara-Terra

Cç da Tapada

Santos

Av 24 de Julho

SANTOS

Get lost in art at the **Museu Nacional de Arte Antiga** (p65)
2 hours

Rio Tejo

Doca de Alcântara

Gain a different perspective on this seafaring metropolis by taking the ferry to **Trafaria** (p74)
½ day

Ponte 25 de Abril

Snap up typical Portuguese wares at **A Vida Portuguesa** (p67)

1 hour

Dance the night away at Lisbon's perennial favourite nightspot **Lux-Frágil** (p61)

1 night

Attend a fado performance at **A Tasca do Chico** (p63)

2 hours

Scale the city's peaks via a variety of methods, such as the **Ascensor da Bica** (p77)

½ hour

Practicalities

FINN STOCK/SHUTTERSTOCK ©

ARRIVING

Humberto Delgado Airport, located just 7km from the city centre, is a short and cheap cab or Uber ride, or even cheaper but slower subway ride, from the main neighbourhoods of interest. The subway, which costs just €1.80 for a single-ride ticket, is located almost directly beneath Terminal 1, which is used by most major airlines. (The bleak, warehouse-like Terminal 2 is used by low-cost carriers.)

HOW MUCH FOR A

Galão (latte) €1.50

Wine at a kiosk €3

Round of Azeitão cheese €5

WHEN TO GO

JAN–MAR

Chilly, sometimes rainy, but a good time to avoid the crowds

APR–JUN

Longer, brighter days and warmer weather

JUL–SEP

High tourist season, but some local businesses shut

OCT–DEC

The rainiest months of the year

GETTING AROUND

Walking is indisputably the best way to navigate Lisbon, though the city does have a decent – and expanding – metro system, as well as its hallmark tramways.

Subway doesn't yet serve all the central neighbourhoods, but is excellent if you're venturing a bit further afield.

Tramway 28E, the iconic route, runs from Mouraria to Campo de Ourique and can get quite crowded, but there are several other tram lines in Lisbon. Don't take the tram if you're in a hurry, as it's not uncommon for them to get trapped behind a poorly parked car or other obstacle.

EATING & DRINKING

Lisbon's cuisine revolves around fish, hearty bean dishes and lots of carbs, especially rice. *Lisboetas* love steaks. They are also fond of salads, ostensibly the origin of their other nickname, *alfacinhas* ('little lettuces'). Lisbon is the origin of many of Portugal's *petiscos* – small dishes paired with drinks. And although it's not as well known as Portugal's other wine regions, the greater Lisbon area produces some deliciously crisp, saline whitaes.

Best introduction to Lisbon dishes **Pica-Pau** (p78)

Best seafood **Cervejaria Ramiro** (p78)

Best custard tarts **Antiga Confeitaria de Belém** (pictured top right; p79)

CONNECT & FIND YOUR WAY

Wi-fi Most European cell phone plans include data roaming in Portugal. For those without a European plan, it's worth getting a SIM card on a prepaid plan from one of the country's three operators: Vodafone, MEO or NOS. Thirty-day plans cost around €20 for 5GB of data.

Navigation With its narrow winding streets, Lisbon is hard to parse without the help of a navigation app.

WHERE TO STAY

Central Lisbon is fairly compact, meaning that you can move easily from one neighbourhood to the next.

Neighbourhood	Pros/Cons
Alfama	This dense warren of little streets is among Lisbon's most picturesque areas, and its most popular.
Bairro Alto	Lisbon's party central, this is the place to be if going out is your main focus.
Chiado	This gorgeous central neighbourhood is among the city's chicest and most expensive.
Campo de Ourique	A bit further out, this neighbourhood offers many of the advantages of Chiado at a lower price.
Arroios	This once rough neighbourhood now offers one of the best quality-to-price ratios in the city.

SENSIBLE SHOES

Be sure to wear shoes with grippy soles, as Lisbon's mosaic sidewalks – known as *calçada portuguesa* – are slippery, and injuries are common.

MONEY

Carry cash – preferably small bills – as some restaurants still don't accept cards, and getting change for bigger bills is a perennial problem.

01 Eating LISBON

SEAFOOD | RUSTIC | DIVERSE

Restaurants in Lisbon run the gamut from the simplest *tascas* (taverns), where both the decor and the prices appear untouched by the passage of time, to Michelin-starred delicacies served up in erstwhile palaces. A common thread is a love of seafood and carbs.

GREG ELMS/LONELY PLANET ©

How to

Not all restaurants accept cards Play it safe by going out armed with cash.

The early bird gets the dinner worm Many *tascas* don't accept reservations; to avoid long queues, it can be a good idea to arrive early.

Appetisers aren't free! Tuck into that spread that's been laid out on the table, and you may find a steep fee tacked on to your bill. Send them back untouched if you don't want them.

BESTRAVELVIDEO/SHUTTERSTOCK ©

SALVADOR AZNAR/SHUTTERSTOCK ©

There are several types of eateries in Lisbon.

Quiosques Lisbon is home to more than two dozen Art Nouveau kiosks, many of which serve snacks in addition to coffee and other drinks, including beer and wine.

Snack bars Areas with lots of foot traffic see snack bars, which serve cheap, quick, deep-fried savoury snacks and sandwiches. Eating at these places is often done standing up, at the counter.

Pastelarias Most *lisboetas* start the day with a roll or pastry and a coffee at one of the city's seemingly countless pastry shops. In addition to pastries, many also serve simple, inexpensive meals. You can eat at the counter or order from the table.

Tascas These unassuming restaurants serve up multi-course, often hearty meals that are usually so much more than the sum of their simple parts – sometimes for as little as €9.

Marisqueiras & cervejarias There's lots of crossover between Lisbon's seafood restaurants (*marisqueiras*) and its beer halls (*cervejarias*), both of which specialise in high-quality seafood and inexpensive beer. A staple at both is the *prego*, Portugal's traditional steak sandwich that's seared and studded with garlic.

Restaurantes In Lisbon, a restaurant typically means a white tablecloth and wine list.

Left Al fresco dining, Chiado neighbourhood **Far left top** A Brasileira (p79), Chiado **Far left bottom** Grilled sardines

Vegans & Vegetarians

Despite the fact that Portuguese food is generally some form of meat and potatoes (or, perhaps more accurately, fish and potatoes), Lisbon's vegan and vegetarian offerings have mushroomed (pun intended) in recent years. Nowadays you'll find meat-free options at lots of traveller-oriented restaurants in central Lisbon, while **arkhe** has taken Portuguese vegetarian cuisine to a new level.

If you're avoiding meat, a ubiquitous go-to is the vegetable-based soups available at just about every pastry shop, snack bar and restaurant in the city. There are also many South Asian–run restaurants in the city that serve meat-free dishes.

THE FLAVOURS
of Lisbon

01 Pastel de Nata
One of Portugal's most famous exports, egg tarts allegedly got their start in Belém, right next door to Lisbon.

02 Bacalhau à Brás
Salt-cod scrambled with eggs and matchstick potatoes is a contemporary classic that was invented by the eponymous chef in Lisbon.

03 Ameijoas à Bulhão Pato
The ideal Lisbon-style *petisco* (snack). Clams – ideally from the Tejo estuary – are cooked with garlic and coriander, and squeezed with lemon juice before serving.

04 Peixinhos da Horta
These battered and deep-fried vegetables – typically green beans – were most likely the inspiration for Japan's tempura.

05 Cachupa
This hominy stew, a staple of the island nation and former Portuguese colony of Cabo Verde, has been adopted by the residents of Lisbon.

06 Açorda de Gambas
Bread soup is an insuffi-

cient name for this mix of stale bread, coriander, garlic, shrimp and broth whipped with egg.

07 Bola de Berlim
Although the name references Berlin, egg-cream donuts are beach fare in Portugal, especially in Lisbon.

08 Caril de Frango
With origins in Goa, India, chicken curry first arrived in Portugal's African colonies before eventually making its way to Lisbon via Portuguese chefs and cooks.

09 Ginjinha
Sour cherry liqueur, typically made in Óbidos, is a common drink in Lisbon, and is sold from centuries-old bars.

10 Sardinhas Assadas
Lisboetas eat grilled sardines all year, but they're especially in demand during the citywide *santos populares* festivities in June.

11 Pica-Pau
Meaning 'woodpecker', allegedly because it's eaten with toothpicks, this drinking snack takes the form of seared cubes of meat in a rich beer- or wine-based sauce.

02 From Dusk TILL DAWN

CHILL | FAR-FLUNG | HEARTFELT

Lisbon's trademark laid-back attitude extends to its nightlife. While the stakes are definitely lower here than in some other European capitals, there's something for almost everyone, from a club where some of the world's top DJs spin to intimate venues serving up everything from fado to Brazilian bossa nova to Angolan *kuduro*.

FINN STOCK/SHUTTERSTOCK ©

How to

Getting around Because central Lisbon is so small and safe, bar-hopping is best done on foot.

When to go While the Portuguese are not as extreme night owls as their Spanish neighbours, venues in Lisbon close relatively late, at around 3am or 4am for bars and 6am for clubs.

Watch the footwear If you plan to check out multiple bars, wear shoes that can handle the mosaic sidewalks (not heels!).

VERONICKA/SHUTTERSTOCK ©

A typical *lisboeta* night out often involves several very different types of experiences, rolled into one. For a perfect start, watch the sunset over a glass of Portuguese wine in one of the many *miradouros* (lookouts), the parks and plazas perched atop Lisbon's myriad hills that boast enviable views over the pastel cityscape. (Legend has it the city was originally built atop seven hills, but a few days of hoofing it up and down Lisbon's seemingly endless peaks and valleys will suffice to make it feel as if the hills number in the hundreds!)

HEMIS/ALAMY STOCK PHOTO ©

Old-school charm Take a dip into the Lisbon of old with a cocktail at one of the charming historic bars, their interiors apparently untouched for decades. In Príncipe Real, try the **Pavilhão Chinês**, its walls lined with a dizzying array of artfully

Lisbon Nightlife

Lisbon may be a small city, but the whole world is here. There's also a huge diversity in the type of experiences available here – with the simplest and most humble venues to the most sophisticated ones.

Mikas, owner of the Social B bar. *@socialb_lisboa*

Left Casa de Linhares (p60), Alfama
Above left Evening streetscape, Lisbon
Above right Yellow and red sangria

displayed old objects, or the red-velvet-swathed **Foxtrot**. **Pensão Amor**, a brothel-turned-bar in the former red-light district and now nightlife-hotspot Cais do Sodré, is another great option.

Live music In the Cais do Sodré district, your choices multiply vertiginously. In the mood for live music? Perfect. But what kind of music? **B.Leza** serves up live Brazilian and African tunes in a raucous, crowded, club-like setting. For similarly eclectic offerings in a much more intimate space, try **Tejo Bar**, a musicians' favourite where many of the sets seem to bubble up spontaneously, and the bargoers show their appreciation – and their respect for the neighbours – not by clapping but rather by rubbing their hands together silently. While fado is sometimes on offer at Tejo Bar, to be sure you don't miss out on the quintessential *lisboêta* musical style, head to **Casa de Linhares**. While most *casas de fado* offer a

Santos Populares

Without doubt Lisbon's most famed street celebration is *santos populares*. Held in honour of St Anthony and St Vincent, Lisbon's historic neighbourhoods fill up with a beer-holding, sardine-eating crowd who dance the night away to a particular Portuguese music genre known as *música pimba* (imagine flashy dancers, high-pitched singers and tunes that mix pop with a folksy beat).

That's the daily (or rather, nightly) top activity during the month of June, peaking on the 13th, which is a holiday in Lisbon. The feast spreads across the city, but it's strongest in Alfama, Graça and Mouraria.

Left *Santos Populares* festivities
Below Pavilhão Chinês (p59)

prix fixe meal that includes the show, at most you can also sneak into the bar after the meal service to revel in the gut-wrenching spectacle over a glass of wine.

Big night out Night owls can make the evening last by heading to one of the neighbourhood clubs. Top choices include **Musicbox**, which has hip-hop nights, and **Incógnito**, a favourite for indie-music lovers. **Lux-Frágil**, which offers revellers the choice of different types of music on different floors, as well as an outsized terrace, has long held the title of Lisbon's top club, regularly attracting some of the world's biggest-name DJs.

The Sound of Longing

MUSIC THAT PLUMBS THE PORTUGUESE SOUL

When singer Amália Rodrigues died in 1999, Portugal's prime minister declared three days of national mourning. It's hard to envisage another performer commanding such a grand final gesture, but over her 50-year career, Rodrigues had grown into an uncontested national treasure – a living symbol of one of the most uniquely Portuguese of art forms: fado.

Left Fado performers, Alfama
Centre Fado restaurant
Right Museu do Fado

JACEK_SOPOTNICKI/GETTY IMAGES ©

Widely compared to Spain's national music, flamenco, fado is darker, rawer and more heartrending than its raucous Spanish cousin. It's also regarded by many Portuguese as a melodic embodiment to the often-brooding and melancholic national character. Traditionally consisting of a single, usually female, singer accompanied by a 12-string Portuguese guitar, fado plumbs the depths of what the Portuguese refer to as *saudade* – a feeling that Portuguese speakers almost defiantly insist has no precise English translation but is essentially an amalgam of homesickness, yearning, sadness and resignation. What fado lacks in upbeat cheer, it makes up for in depth of feeling.

Emerging in the early 19th century in the riverside neighbourhoods of central Lisbon, fado was initially the music of the disenfranchised – of pimps and sex workers, petty criminals and day labourers, and also of the sailors from the world over who dropped anchor in the city. It gradually grew in popularity and moved out of brothels and flophouses and into more 'respectable' venues. With the 1926 military coup that ushered in the authoritarian dictatorship of António Salazar, fado became increasingly institutionalised, with a fixed repertoire and performances in so-called *casas de fado* (houses of fado), many of them concentrated in Lisboa's Bairro Alto and some of which are still around today. Because it had been embraced by Salazar, whose slogan was Deus, Pátria e Família (God, Country and Family), fado would be widely rejected by younger generations following the 1974 Carnation Revolution that brought the nearly half-century-long regime to an end.

AMNAT30/SHUTTERSTOCK ©

SOPOTNICKI/SHUTTERSTOCK ©

Where to Revel in the Saudade

For a deeper dive into the history of fado, check out the Museu do Fado, in Alfama, which traces its emergence as the quintessential Portuguese musical genre. Chock-a-block with fado-related memorabilia, the museum makes for a good preamble to some of the nearby *casas de fado*. There are literally dozens of such venues, some more authentic, upscale or kitsch than others. Among the most prestigious is the Mesa de Frades (Rua dos Remédios 139), where some of the most acclaimed contemporary fado acts perform regularly.

> Fado was initially the music of the disenfranchised – of pimps and sex workers, petty criminals and day labourers, and of the sailors from the world over who dropped anchor in the city.

Fado Today

Largely eschewed by Baby Boomers, who were on the front lines of the Carnation Revolution, fado has been embraced by successive generations, and now top performers and fans make up a diverse group that includes many with roots in Portugal's former colonies. This new generation of *fadistas* (fado singers), among them the Grammy-nominated singer Mariza, has injected a stiff dose of innovation and experimentation, pushing the envelope of traditional fado by incorporating a diverse array of instruments and musical influences. Many of these new *fadistas* have also pushed back against the sober black costumes and are taking to the stage in colourful, exuberant and even, gasp, occasionally sexy looks.

Casas de Fado

A Tasca do Chico The Alfama branch of this legend, combining soulful fado and a decent dinner, is a great introduction to the genre.

Adega Machado A fixture of the Bairro Alto since 1937, it's a favourite of hardcore fado fans.

O Faia Another top *casa de fado* in the Bairro Alto, O Faia has played host to many of the biggest names in fado, past and present.

Senhor Vinho A much newer addition to the fado scene – it was founded in 1975 – Senhor Vinho is the night owls' favourite, with its kitchen that stays open till midnight.

03 Stroll the Lisbon OF OLD

RETRO | AUTHENTIC | HIP

While Lisbon has busily set about reinventing itself since it emerged as a hot tourist destination over the past few years, much of the city's appeal resides in its old-school charm – which lives on, largely undisturbed, in Alcântara.

RIBEIROANTONIO/SHUTTERSTOCK ©

Trip Notes

Getting here Take the 15E tram, which leaves from the central Praça da Figueira and extends all the way to the far-western neighbourhood of Algés.

When to go Because the beauty of this place lies in its exquisite ordinariness, any old day is a good one to visit!

History Once exurban farmland, Alcântara was eventually absorbed into Lisbon and later became a textiles hub before succumbing to deindustrialisation. Shielded by a rough reputation, Alcântara largely avoided the recent wave of gentrification, making it the perfect place to take in the Lisbon of old.

Saving History

'Lisbon is a unique, historic city. But it's changing so fast,' notes Helena Espvall, who has spearheaded a campaign to save a crumbling 19th-century mansion on her street, Rua dos Lusíadas, which was slated to be turned into a hotel.

Helena Espvall, Swedish-born musician and Alcântara resident. *@helenaespvall*

02 This industrial complex once housed a printing press and a textile plant but now **LX Factory** is a buzzing hive of clothing and jewellery stores, co-working spaces, bookshops, and hip restaurants and bars.

03 Get a taste of the Alentejo region at **Solar dos Nunes**, a high-end, family-run restaurant that has been written up in the *Michelin Guide* and has garnered a celebrity clientele.

Built in 1549, **Capela Santo Amaro** (pictured left) has fantastic work and, perched op a hill, offers a ivileged view out over e Tagus and the nearby nte 25 de Abril – sbon's answer to the lden Gate Bridge.

01 Start the tour just outside the eastern edge of Alcântara, in Lapa, at the unmissable **Museu Nacional de Arte Antiga**. Housed in a 17th-century palace, the museum has an unbeatable collection of Portuguese art, as well as treasures from former colonies from Brazil to Japan.

05 For a closer look at the Ponte 25 de Abril from 80m above ground, and to be wowed by this feat of engineering, check out **Experiência Pilar 7**.

Parque Florestal de Monsanto

Tapada das Necessidades

Tapada da Ajuda

Av da Ponte

Av de Ceuta

Alcântara- Terra

Av Infante Santo

LAPA

Cç da Tapada

R dos Lusíadas

R Primeiro de Maio

Av 24 de Julho

R Presidente Arriaga

ALCÂNTARA

Alcântara-Mar

Doca de Alcântara

Doca de Santo Amaro

Av da Índia

Rio Tejo

Ponte 25 de Abril

0 1 km

0 0.5 miles

04 Made in PORTUGAL

HANDICRAFTS | ARTISANS | TRADITION

Portugal is one of the last remaining enclaves of artisanal savoir faire in Europe. Here, you can still find craftspeople making everything from ceramics and leather goods to baskets, hand-spun wool and furniture the old way – according to traditional, or even millennial, techniques.

INGEHOGENBIJL/SHUTTERSTOCK ©

How to

Seek out artisans Outdoor fairs that are often held in parks are a great place to connect with local makers.

Carry cash Otherwise you might find yourself searching for an ATM.

Out for lunch Some stores, particularly small family-run shops, still follow the Old World tradition of closing during lunchtime, and some are only open until around noon on Saturdays.

GREG ELMS/LONELY PLANET ©

CRISTINA ARIAS/GETTY IMAGES ©

Left A Vida Portuguesa **Far left top** Portuguese ceramics **Far left bottom** Feira da Ladra

Major international fashion labels come to Portugal to source the kind of handiwork that is nearly impossible to find elsewhere. Give those labels a pass and instead, head straight to **A Vida Portuguesa**, a one-stop-shop for all things Made in Portugal. This is one of Lisbon's coolest and most unique shops, as it brings together some of the best handicrafts from around the country, along with quintessentially old-school Portuguese brands whose products and packaging have remained unchanged for decades. It might sound kitsch, and probably would be if everything weren't so appealingly curated and artfully displayed.

The store has two Lisbon locations, and they're so perfect that you can't help but want to snap up just about everything. Ever imagined that you needed a soup bowl shaped like a cabbage leaf, made by the storied Portuguese ceramics maker Bordalo Pinheiro? Or do you fancy a pair of hand-tooled leather clogs, or maybe some silver polish that comes in a cute metal tin? Also make sure and keep an eye out for the store's selection of fancy soaps and perfumes from Claus Porto, the historic soap brand that has its own standalone shop on Rua da Misericordia.

With three branches along Rua Augusto Rosa opposite the Sé Cathedral, **Chi Coração** also offers an excellent selection of real Portuguese handicrafts, unlike the imported, mass-produced simulacra that fill the city's trinket shops.

Feira da Ladra

There's no end to the treasures on offer at the Feira da Ladra (which literally – and appropriately – translates as Thieves' Market), but be aware that you'll have sift through a fair amount of what can only be described as junk to find it. Bring small bills, as change is a perennial problem. Just don't give into the temptation of buying tiles at the Feira da Ladra, as some have been illegally ripped off buildings. If you feel an overwhelming urge to take home a Portuguese tile or two, head to an authorised dealer, such as **d'Orey Azulejos**, on Rua do Alecrim, where the wares are legitimately sourced.

05 Historic LISBON

IMPRESSIVE | FRAUGHT | OMNIPRESENT

Lisbon is Europe's second-oldest city, after Athens, so history is everywhere you look. There are the remains of a Roman amphitheatre dating from 57 CE and numerous gorgeous old churches, as well as the setting-off point for many of the maritime explorations that would see the Portuguese flag planted across three continents. There are even the remnants of a 20-million-year-old coral reef!

MILOSK50/SHUTTERSTOCK ©

How to

Getting here Belém is quite a hike from central Lisbon, so kill two birds with one stone and experience one of Lisbon's famed trams by taking the 15E line.

When to go During the summer tourist high season, queues at historic sites can be daunting; visit during spring or autumn if possible.

Call ahead Visits to some sites, particularly those that are privately owned, must be booked in advance. It's generally best to call ahead to check.

CHRISDORNEY/SHUTTERSTOCK ©

Left Mosteiro dos Jerónimos **Far left top** Igreja de São Domingos **Far left bottom** Convento do Carmo

The Earthquake of 1755

No single event marked both the geography and psychology of the city as deeply as the devastating 1755 earthquake, which was followed by a tidal wave and deadly fires. Memories of the traumatic triple-whammy catastrophe, which flattened much of the old city, remain deeply imprinted on the collective consciousness. To get a sense of the devastation wrought, check out the **Convento do Carmo**, the ruins of a Gothic monastery that was destroyed in the quake.

Another of the sites lost in the earthquake was the Paço da Ribeira, the extravagant royal palace that was built in what is now the Praça do Comércio during the Age of Discovery and was said to contain incalculable treasures. Still, its replacement, the **Palácio Nacional da Ajuda** – in the western Ajuda neighbourhood, to which the royal family decamped after the disaster – is open to the public and well worth the visit.

The hub of Age of Discovery sites is **Belém**, the western Lisbon neighbourhood situated along the Tagus River, from where many maritime expeditions set sail. Two of the main symbols of the period, the **Torre de Belém**, a four-storey-tall river fortification, and the nearby **Mosteiro dos Jerónimos**, a Gothic monastery that was constructed shortly after Vasco da Gama's historic 1498 voyage to India, came through the 1755 earthquake remarkably unscathed.

The Churches of Lisbon

With some 120 churches – many of them built during the heyday of Portuguese wealth – there are plenty of breathtaking options to choose from, including these two standouts.

Igreja de São Domingos
This marred beauty in the Santa Maria Maior neighbourhood has known tragedy in the form of floods, earthquakes and, finally, a devastating 1959 fire that makes it unlike any other church you've ever seen.

Igreja de São Roque This baroque masterpiece survived the 1755 earthquake with hardly a scratch and is indisputably one of the most jaw-dropping churches in the city.

A Proud but Fraught History

PORTUGUESE EXPLORERS HAVE COME UNDER SCRUTINY

The Portuguese take great pride in the feats of their forebears, the intrepid navigators who, starting in the early 15th century, set sail for parts unknown, eventually claiming vast swathes of land stretching from South America all the way to East Asia.

Left Padrão dos Descobrimentos (Monument to the Discoveries) **Centre** Vasco da Gama **Right** *Mappa mundi* fragment, Padrão dos Descobrimentos

PAULSAT/SHUTTERSTOCK ©

A Globe-Spanning Empire

Centuries before the British, the Portuguese had already built an empire upon which the sun never set: after claiming Ceuta (the now-Spanish enclave in present-day Morocco) in 1415, a series of Portuguese navigators spent the first half of the 15th century working their way down the western coast of Africa in search of new trade routes and 'discovering' a series of islands along the way, including Madeira and Cape Verde. Vasco da Gama reached India's western coast just years ahead of Pedro Álvarez Cabral's 1500 arrival in Brazil. Portugal's Diogo Ziemoto is said to be one of the first Europeans to alight in Japan, in 1542.

'The Portuguese started something that radically changed the history of the world,' said historian João Paulo Oliveira e Costa, a professor at the Universidade Nova de Lisboa and the author of more than a dozen books on the Portuguese expansion. 'The Age of Discovery was, by any measure, indisputably positive for humanity.'

Portugal's Role in Enslavement

But a growing cadre of academics, journalists, artists and activists are questioning the supposed gloriousness of the Age of Discovery and reexamining the role Portugal's empire played in the enslavement of millions of African people.

Portugal instigated the Atlantic trade of enslaved people – which began in 1444 – with the sale in the southern Portuguese city of Lagos of more than 200 people who were trafficked from the coast of West Africa. Over the next 400 years, Portuguese vessels transported an estimated 5.8 million enslaved Africans across the Atlantic.

TONYBAGGETT/GETTY IMAGES ©

DAMIRA/SHUTTERSTOCK ©

By contrast, Portugal's nearest rival in the trade of enslaved people, the British, are estimated to have transported some 3.2 million enslaved Africans, according to the Trans-Atlantic Slave Trade Database, a collaborative project that draws on data from around the world to tally the scope of the tragic human commerce. (See slavevoyages.org for more info.)

> A growing cadre of academics, journalists, artists and activists are questioning the supposed gloriousness of the Age of Discovery.

Memorialising the Past

While the vast majority of enslaved Africans sold by the Portuguese ended up in Brazil – the country's mammoth South American colony – the practice of 'owning' enslaved people was also widespread in Portugal itself. It's estimated that as early as the 16th century, one out of every 10 Lisbon residents was an enslaved African. And yet, Lisbon has never had a monument honouring enslaved peoples' historic contribution to the city, nor one marking Portugal's role in the horrific trade of enslaved people.

However, in 2017, the city's residents approved a memorial to enslaved people. Imagined by Angolan artist Kiluanji Kia Henda, the memorial will turn Lisbon's central Praça das Cebolas into a 'sugarcane' plantation, made up of 560 stalks of black aluminium – in a nod to the 'white gold' that helped Europe to prosper at the expense of millions of enslaved people. The memorial will constitute Portugal's most significant mea culpa to date for its role in the Trans-Atlantic Slave Trade.

The Myth of the 'Bons Colonizadores'

'The myth that the Portuguese colonial expansion was something benign, the "first globalisation", is everywhere in Portugal – spread not only in our schools, but also on TV, in advertising, in the monuments that dot our cities. It's crucial we dismantle those myths,' said Beatriz Gomes Dias, a councillor, lawmaker and one of three Black women to serve in the Portuguese parliament when she was elected in 2019. 'Even though we of course cannot change what happened in the past, we can change the way we speak about that history today. And that will change the way we act in the present.'

■ **Beatriz Gomes Dias**, Lisbon City Council

06 Hidden GEMS

GARDENS | MARKETS | MUSEUMS

While it may feel like a village, Lisbon is a city of 2.8 million inhabitants – with the vast majority of the metropolis generally off the beaten path. But venture even further afield and you can find the hidden treasures that make this city truly unique.

LUIS VASCONCELOS/GETTY IMAGES/500PX ©

 **How to**

Getting around Use the metro to get to more distant points of interest. Clean, cheap and efficient, Lisbon's metro works best for covering longer distances.

When to go While Lisbon has plenty of must-sees, devote one day out of a week-long visit to checking out spots off the beaten track.

Stay aware Walking around alone at night can feel unsafe in Lisbon's empty and poorly lit streets.

MICAEL NUSSBAUMER/SHUTTERSTOCK ©

Lisbon's discretion and laid-back attitude extends to many of its most interesting spots. Sure, there are a few downright remarkable places – including the Tile Museum and the Oceanário aquarium, as well as the rickety but iconic Number 28 tramline – that get all the attention, but there are also a slew of really interesting sites that fly under the radar, not only of most visitors but even of many residents.

Museu do Traje One such place is the Museu Nacional do Traje (Costume Museum), which traces the evolution of Portuguese fashion from the 17th century to the present day. Located in a former aristocratic mansion in the northern neighbourhood of Lumiar, the museum is a fun visit even for those who couldn't care less about clothing thanks to its sumptuous, sculpture-studded

TISHA RAZUMOVSKY/SHUTTERSTOCK ©

 **Shop Like a Local**

Skip the supermarket at the **Mercado de Benfica** in the working-class neighbourhood of the same name. The iconic domed market is particularly revered for its seafood, but it's a microcosm of Portuguese gastronomy, with vegetables, fruit, bread, cheese and meats, as well as products from the greater Lusophone world.

Above left Reservatório da Mãe d'Água das Amoreiras (p75) **Left** Jardim Botânico Tropical de Lisboa (p74) **Above right** Metro station, Lisbon

grounds and quirky restaurant. It's a wonderful spot for an afternoon pick-me-up and leisurely stroll through the garden for both clothes horses and the fashion averse alike.

Jardim Botânico Tropical de Lisboa
Not to be confused with any of the city's multiple other botanical gardens, the Jardim Botânico Tropical de Lisboa is a lush enclave in Belém that's so rife with tropical flora brought back from Portugal's former colonies it's said to have its own microclimate. But it also has a dark past: in 1940, under the regime of dictator António Salazar, it was the site of a human zoo, with the Portuguese public lining up to gawk at whole families snatched from their homes in Guinea-Bissau and other Portuguese territories in Africa. This is clearly not something the management is interested in highlighting – the information pamphlet makes no mention of the shameful incident – and the busts of African men and women

Ferry Back in Time to Trafaria

Just a 20-minute ferry ride away from Belém, Trafaria feels distant, both geographically and temporally. The town retains the feel of the fishing village it used to be, and a stroll around the streets, with its motley fleet of wooden boats and picturesque collection of weather-beaten buildings, plunges visitors back into Portugal's not-so-distant past. What Trafaria lacks in must-visit sites it makes up for in vivid character. Plus, if you rent a bike from a stand near the ferry terminal in Belém, you can cycle from Trafaria to São João da Caparica, and from there down the coast.

Left Ferry disembarkation, Trafaria
Below Sculpture, Jardim Botânico Tropical de Lisboa

that dot the grounds are the only hints of that little-known history.

Reservatório da Mãe d'Água das Amoreiras A site whose name literally translates as 'the mother of waters' might sound like a strange place to visit, and indeed this 18th-century water reservoir might initially seem like a quirky choice. But with its gorgeous arched ceilings, placid pools and verdant fountains, this landmark on the equally beautiful Praça das Amoreiras, where the city's silk weavers were once concentrated, is not only a key part of Lisbon's history, but also just a beautiful spot to take in something weird and wonderful.

Igreja do Convento dos Cardaes You could probably walk by the plain facade of the Cardaes Convent hundreds of times without suspecting that behind the walls lies an opulent, gold- and tile-drenched gem. Built in the 17th century, and showcasing not only the sheer wealth but also the actual gold that was extracted from Brazil, this convent survived the 1755 quake largely unscathed.

07 Scaling Lisbon's PEAKS

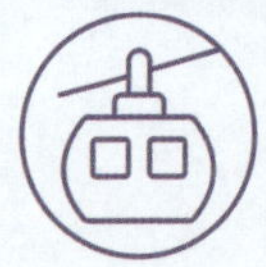

ARCHITECTURE | HISTORY | ACTIVITY

Over the centuries, Lisbon's city planners have devised a number of creative ways to ascend the city's seven hills. The various ways - old and new, free and paid - of tackling the Lisbon's challenging geography are sure to provide you with a new perspective on the city.

KERRY MURRAY/LONELY PLANET ©

Trip Notes

When to go During the peak tourist months, the queues for Elevador de Santa Justa can be very long.

Tickets Single-ride fares on Lisbon's funiculars are disproportionally expensive; buy a single- or multi-day card to save cash.

A new generation These days, tourists form the vast majority of passengers on the city's funiculars.

Free Ride

The 287 Escadinhas do Saúde ('Healthy Stairs') connect Martim Moniz and Mouraria. A free escalator runs parallel – when it works.

The Baixa-Chiado metro escalators escort you to Chiado.

The Elevador Castelo-Baixa leads to the Elevador Castelo. The entrance is hidden in the Pingo Doce grocery store.

04 Elevador da Glória This funicular helps *lisboetas* shortcut the steep climb connecting Praça dos Restauradores to Bairro Alto in less than five minutes.

05 Ascensor do Lavra This is the first street funicular in the world, in operation since 1884. The trip lasts less than two minutes, but it beats tackling the steep 188m of Calçada do Lavra on foot.

03 Ascensor da Bica This funicular (pictured left) connects Rua de São Paulo (Cais do Sodré) to Rua do Loreto (Bairro Alto).

02 Elétrico 28E The most famous of Lisbon's yellow trams, the 28E, runs from Martim Moniz to Campo de Ourique.

01 Elevador de Santa Justa Lisbon's most iconic lift was inaugurated in 1902, and carries passengers the 45 vertical metres from Baixa to Chiado.

Listings

BEST OF THE REST

Local Faves & Far-Flung Flavours

Cervejaria Ramiro €€€

Opened in 1956, Ramiro has legendary status among Lisbon's seafood lovers, and is one of the country's most famous restaurants. Come here for simple, excellent seafood.

Prado €€€

This high-end restaurant, helmed by talented young chef António Galapito, is seasonally driven and emphasises locally sourced ingredients. A clever choice for your splurge meal.

Essencial €€€

For refined, French-inspired food in a chic setting, try this small Bairro Alto restaurant.

Canalha €€€

It's worth the schlep to Belém for chef João Rodrigues' simple yet sublime dishes that blur the lines between Spain and Portugal.

Pica-Pau €€

This cosy-feeling Príncipe Real restaurant serves as an excellent crash course in Lisbon-style dishes and dining; book in advance.

Último Porto €€

This restaurant on the Doca de Alcântara boasts solid seafood at reasonable prices and great views onto the Tagus; a real Lisbon institution.

Pigmeu €€

Pork-centred, nose-to-tail cooking is the emphasis at this delicious Campo de Ourique spot, but veggies and intriguing wines also make regular appearances.

O Velho Eurico €€

A young-feeling Portuguese restaurant that nonetheless maintains the vibe of a classic *taberna* (simple restaurant); great for a raucous night out.

Zé da Mouraria €€

No-reservation traditional Portuguese eatery serving comically hearty portions in the heart of Mouraria. Lunch only.

A Provinciana €

Massive servings, cheeky service, and wine barrels as interior design: Rossio's A Provinciana is the dictionary-definition *tasca*.

Taberna Albricoque €€

This restaurant near Santa Apolónia station specialises in the dishes of the Algarve; a great research meal before your trip south.

Antiga Camponesa €€

Classic dishes that veer off in smart, subtle and occasionally international directions are the centrepiece of this Chiado restaurant.

Tasca Baldracca €€

Brazilian chef Pedro Monteiro oversees this fresh, fun, eclectic take on the Lisbon *tasca*. Located in Mouraria.

A Brasileira

Acarajé da Carol €

The eponymous owner here has brought black-eyed pea fritters from her home in Bahia, Brazil, to Bairro Alto.

Fox Coffee €

The name here is a red herring for one of Lisbon's best bowls of *cachupa*, a hearty hominy-based stew with origins in the former Portuguese colony of Cape Verde.

Sipping & Snacking

Casa São Miguel €

Located in the heart of Alfama, this retro-themed tea and coffee salon boasts a glass case packed with Portuguese sweets from just about every corner of the country.

Confeitaria Nacional €

In Baixa since 1829, this Lisbon legend is a crash course in local pastries and sweets.

Alcôa €

This pastry shop in Chiado brings together traditional, handmade sweets from a convent in central Portugal.

Juliana Penteado Pastry €

For something sweet yet contemporary, head to this showcase of fantastical creations from the eponymous Brazilian pastry chef.

Bettina & Niccolò Corallo €

This family-run transplant from São Tomé and Príncipe elicits enthusiasm for its artisan chocolates, coffee, ice creams and sorbets.

Antiga Confeitaria de Belém €

In operation since 1837, this bakery in Belém claims to be the origin of the *pastel de nata*, or custard tart.

Atelier Pudim Rei €

Chef Miguel Oliveira does what is arguably one of the country's best versions of *pudim Abade de Priscos*, a hyper-decadent sweet combining egg yolks, pork fat, sugar, port wine and aromatics. Located near the Marquês de Pombal roundabout.

SARIONUNES/SHUTTERSTOCK ©

A Ginjinha

A Brasileira €

Everyone eventually ends up at this hauntingly beautiful, exceedingly popular 1905-era cafe, right in the heart of Chiado.

Distinctive Drinking & Dancing

A Ginjinha €

This stall – don't come expecting seating – in Rossio is Lisbon's most legendary place to try *ginjinha*, aka sour cherry liqueur.

Quiosque de São Paulo €

Art Nouveau–era kiosk selling a selection of once-common drinks that are increasingly hard to find these days, as well as some tasty snacks and light dishes.

Memmo Alfama €€

Alfama unfolds like origami from the stylish roof terrace of the Memmo Alfama hotel. Stop by for the dreamy vistas over the rooftops, spires and the Rio Tejo, and stay for a sundowner.

Vino Vero €€

Located at the top of the hill in Graça is this perpetually packed, Italian-run bar specialising in natural wines.

Liquid Love €€

The bartender-owners' Italian and Cabo Verdean roots are apparent at this sultry cocktail bar just off Avenida Almirante Reis.

Comida Independente €€

Part curated grocery, part wine bar, Comida Independente has a bit of everything for the discerningly hungry and thirsty. Located just west of Cais do Sodré.

Tabernáculo by Hernâni Miguel €€

Born in Guinea-Bissau and raised in Portugal, the owner of this wine bar and gastropub in Cais do Sodré brings together African food, Portuguese wines and Brazilian music.

Black Sheep €€

Knowledgeable and friendly staff pour rare bottles at what is probably the city's best wine bar. Located at Praça das Flores.

Musa da Bica €

The 15 taps here are full of their iconic music-pun pours, including the Eye of the Lager, Born in the IPA and Saison O'Connor.

Damas

Popular with students, this restaurant-bar venue in Graça is also a live-music and event venue showcasing a wide variety of acts.

Incógnito

Pint-sized Chiado-ish club offering an alternative vibe and DJs thrashing out indie rock and electropop.

Architecture, Greenery & Art

Castelo de São Jorge

With sections that date back to the 6th century, this fortress has seen waves of conquerors, including the Romans and the Visigoths, and boasts privileged views of the city.

Mosteiro de São Vicente de Fora

Graça's Mosteiro de São Vicente de Fora boasts elaborate blue-and-white tile murals that dance across almost every wall, echoing the building's architectural curves.

Casa dos Bicos

This 16th-century townhouse near the Terreiro do Paço is a museum honouring the late great Portuguese writer José Saramago, winner of the 1998 Nobel Prize in Literature.

Estufa Fria

This charming greenhouse complex in the Parque Eduardo VII houses botanical gardens filled with flora from different climates.

Escola Portuguesa de Arte Equestre

Portugal's answer to the Spanish Riding School in Vienna, this is an essential visit for horse lovers. In addition to watching the formal performances, you can book in advance to attend one of their daily training sessions.

Cinema Ideal

This little arthouse movie theatre in Chiado boasts the city's best cinematic line-up.

Fundação Calouste Gulbenkian

Nestled in a park, this art museum holds one of the world's largest private collections, assembled by oil baron Calouste Gulbenkian.

Casa dos Bicos

Casa-Museu Medeiros e Almeida

Once the mansion of another gentleman entrepreneur and art collector, this museum off Avenida Liberdade is packed with priceless treasures from around the world.

Fundação das Casas Fronteira e Alorna

Book in advance for a guided tour of the manicured grounds and lavish, tile-covered palace that's still in the hands of the aristocratic family that built it, way back in the 17th century.

Museu de Arte Contemporânea

Culture fiends can get their contemporary-art fix at this Belém museum, where the minimalist gallery displays an eye-popping collection of abstract, surrealist and pop art.

 Antiques, Handicrafts & Gifts

Brisa Galeria

Founded in 2018 by an couple from Rio de Janeiro, this space in Chiado has emerged as one of Lisbon's most interesting galleries.

Companhia Portugueza dos Chás

Tea lovers mustn't miss this tea and tea-accoutrement store that brings together an aromatic selection of loose-leaf teas sourced from around the world; housed in a former shoe shop dating from 1880.

Rua de São Bento

For a dizzying selection of antiques spanning the centuries, head to this street in Estrela, where shop after shop is packed with fascinating finds.

Tania Gil Jewelry

A veritable treasure trove of unique gifts, this little shop in Santos showcases the work of talented young jeweller Tania Gil.

Embaixada

Chapelaria Azevedo Rua

This historic hat shop off the Praça Dom Pedro IV also custom makes a wide variety of high-quality headgear for surprisingly affordable prices.

Filipe Faísca

Among Portugal's top designers, Faísca does inventive contemporary takes on traditional Portuguese garb, like oversized cocoon coats made out of shepherds' blankets and fetching shirts with hand-made lace cutouts.

ICON Shop

The top contemporary designers and makers of all sorts of objects, from ceramics to leather goods to jewellery and textiles, are represented at this store in Chiado.

Restrosaria Rosa Pomar

This knitting supply shop in Bairro Alto is *the* place to go for quality Portuguese yarns.

Embaixada

Housed in a 19th-century neo-Moorish palace, this shopping centre has boutiques selling everything from vintage records to organic cosmetics, eco-homewares, contemporary Portuguese ceramics and catwalk styles.

BEYOND
LISBON
NATURE | HISTORY | CULTURE

Explore the marine life of the **Reserva Natural de Berlengas** (p100)
2 hours from Lisbon

Time-travel to the medieval era in **Óbidos** (p96)
1 hour from Lisbon

Take in the fantastical architecture of **Sintra** (p88)
1 hour from Lisbon

Sunbathe on the dunes of **Tróia** (p95)
2 hours from Lisbon

Say hi to Lisbon's beachy neighbours, **Cascais and Estoril** (p86)
½ hour from Lisbon

Shop at the **Mercado do Livramento** (p93)
1 hour from Lisbon

Enjoy SUP or kayaking in the **Parque Natural da Serra da Arrábida** (p95)
1 hour from Lisbon

Join a boat trip along the **Rio Sado** to spot dolphins (p95)
1 hour from Lisbon

Fátima (Cova da Iria)
Parque Natural das Serras de Aire e Candeeiros
Foz do Arelho
Caldas da Rainha
Peniche
Serra de Montejunto
Rio Tejo
RIBAT
ATLANTIC OCEAN
Parque Natural de Sintra-Cascais
Colares
Rio Tejo
LISBON
Barreiro
Setúbal Peninsula
Sesimbra
Comporta
Río Sado
BAI ALENT
Sines
Parque Nat do Sudoeste Alentejano e Costa Vice
Rio Mira
Cavaleiro
0 50 km
0 25 miles

BEYOND LISBON
Trip Builder

Let your imagination run free with remnants from another time, or allow yourself to be conquered by beaches and mountains alike. Beyond Lisbon, there is a region of good food and fabulous wines, destined to excite even the most jaded of travellers.

Practicalities

ARRIVING

Estação Ferroviária de Sete Rios, in Lisbon, is where the train leaves to Setúbal.

Estação Rodoviária do Campo Grande, also in Lisbon, has buses to Peniche and Óbidos.

FIND YOUR WAY

Look for the Posto de Turismo, which has information about what to see and do.

MONEY

Carry some cash just in case, but credit cards are accepted almost everywhere, and there are numerous ATMs.

WHERE TO STAY

Location	Pros/Cons
Comporta	Chic design hotels close to the beach.
Sintra	Old chalets, century-old manor houses and small apartments.
Setúbal	Cheap options in the centre. Book in advance.
Óbidos	Charming properties in a medieval town.
Berlengas	Surf houses in Peniche, just a boat ride from the islands.

GETTING AROUND

Driving is the best way to visit the cities around Lisbon.

Buses serve spots like Peniche and Óbidos, while trains connect Lisbon with Sintra, Cascais and Estoril.

Ferries connect Lisbon and the Setúbal Peninsula, as well as Tróia and Comporta.

EATING & DRINKING

Wine Although not as famous as the Douro or Alentejo regions, the greater Lisbon area is the source of some amazing wines; seek out those from Colares, Setúbal and Torres Vedras.

Fish Setúbal and Peniche are the spots for fish. With large fishing ports, this is as fresh as it gets.

Dessert The Setúbal Peninsula's *torta de Azeitão* (pictured), a sponge cake filled with egg yolks, is a must-try.

JAN–MAR

Rainy season, ideal for visiting museums and monuments

APR–JUN

Mild temperatures, perfect for outdoor activities

JUL–SEP

Hot and dry weather; the busiest time of the year

OCT–DEC

Temperatures drop; calls for local comfort food

08 Lisbon's NEIGHBOURS

CYCLING | WATER SPORTS | MUSEUMS

The area stretching west from Lisbon, where the Tejo River and the Atlantic Ocean become one, is called the Portuguese Riviera. Perfect waves for surfers, laid-back urban beaches, picturesque lighthouses, grand mansions and attractive towns such as Cascais await.

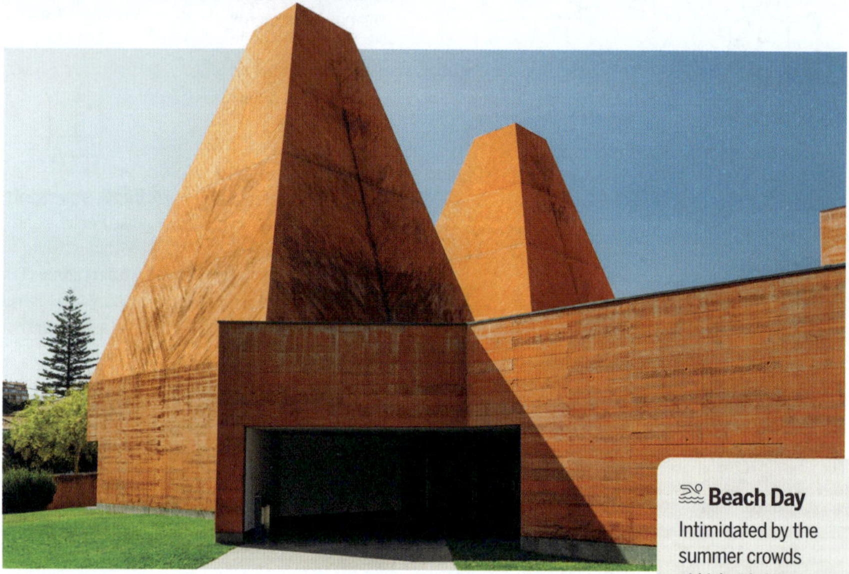

Trip Notes

Getting here Trains to Cascais depart every 20 minutes throughout the day from Lisbon's Cais do Sodré station. Some cars are equipped for bicycle and surfboard storage.

Getting around Bikes can be rented at the MobiCascais kiosk near Cascais train station.

When to go Lisbon beaches can be absolutely packed on summer weekends, so try to keep to the weekdays if possible.

Beach Day

Intimidated by the summer crowds at Lisbon's bigger beaches? Despite being just an easy train ride from the city, tiny **Praia das Avencas** feels wonderfully hidden; it even has an attached bar. It can be reached via train from Lisbon's Cais do Sodré train station.

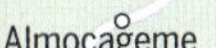

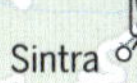

05 Continue along the bike path to **Praia do Guincho**, where perpetually windy conditions mean you're likely to see plenty of windsurfing and kitesurfing.

03 Walk or hop on the train to the former fishing village of Cascais, where you can grab lunch, then stop at **Casa das Histórias** (pictured left) to see the works of Portuguese-born, London-based artist Paula Rego.

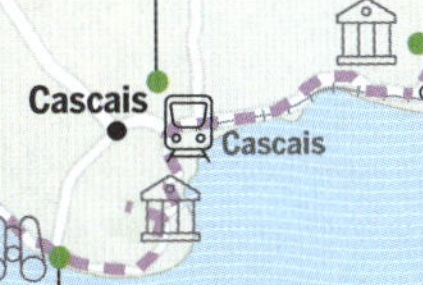

02 From Carcavelos, walk along the coast or take the train to Estoril, where you'll find worthwhile beaches, decadent summer homes and the **Casino Estoril**, which allegedly inspired Ian Fleming's Bond novels.

04 From Cascais, grab a bike and head to **Boca do Inferno**, a site known both for its pounding waves (if the weather is right) and beautiful views.

01 Take the commuter train (grab a seat on the left-hand side for the best views) from **Cais do Sodré** to **Praia de Carcavelos**, probably the most popular Lisbon beach, and one that's good for surfing.

Almoçageme
Sintra
Algueirão-Mem Martins
CRUZ ALTA
Parque Natural de Sintra-Cascais
Malveira
Areia
Alcabideche
Cascais
Estoril
Carcavelos
Parede
Perede
Oeiras
ATLANTIC OCEAN
0 2 km
0 1 mile

BEKETOFF/SHUTTERSTOCK ©
AFONSO NEVES/GETTY IMAGES ©

09 Unknown SINTRA

MONUMENTS | WALKING | NATURE

Sintra was the first place in Europe to be listed by UNESCO as a Cultural Landscape, and it is this very landscape that attracts visitors from all over the world. Sintra is full of lavish palaces, manors and villas, not to mention its imposing castle. Amid the lush scenery of this Portuguese town are numerous secrets worth unravelling.

STEFANO_VALERI/SHUTTERSTOCK ©

How to

Getting here Take the train at Estação do Rossio, in Lisbon. From Sintra station, several buses go to the main monuments. Avoid taking a car into Sintra's historical centre, as several streets have limited access.

When to go Weekdays and low season are your best options. During the summer months and at weekends, the town fills up with visitors.

Hiking There are several trails that cross the natural park and lead to the main monuments of Sintra.

LIFECOLLECTIONPHOTOGRAPHY/SHUTTERSTOCK ©

Left Palácio Nacional da Pena **Far left top** Palácio de Monserrate **Far left bottom** Parque Natural de Sintra-Cascais

Palace tours Sintra's palaces are a must for everyone who visits what is considered the most romantic village in Portugal. But what if you could see them exclusively, just you and your travel companions? Sintra's **Palácio Nacional da Pena** and the **Palácio de Monserrate**, as well as **Palácio Nacional de Queluz** (in Queluz), open their doors after hours for those who want to visit on a private tour, accompanied by experts who know every corner of these historic buildings.

Going backstage There is more to Sintra than meets the eye. Places that are usually closed to the public are now accessible in the company of specialists in the most diverse areas.

Access the interior of the great dome of the yellow tower of Palácio da Pena to see works of art and objects that have never been on display, and climb the clock tower to have one of the best views of this UNESCO World Heritage Site.

Learn about the past and the people who passed through Sintra on a visit to the **Castelo dos Mouros**, guided by the archaeologist responsible for recent excavations.

Follow the tunnels that form the network of water mines that cross the **Parque Natural de Sintra-Cascais** in the company of a historian, or walk through the **Tapada de Monserrate** guided by a biologist who explains the work done to preserve the local ecosystem.

Contact the **Posto de Turismo de Sintra**, Sintra's tourism office, to be connected with private guides and experts who can facilitate these experiences.

Accessible Sintra

As one of the most visited locations in the Lisbon region, Sintra's monuments have adapted to visitors with special needs.

Under the project Parques de Sintra Welcome Better, accessibility improvements include the introduction of ramps and lift platforms, the capacity for wheelchairs in tourist buses, and even the introduction of electric wheelchairs for nature walks, among other things.

Visitors with special needs can also access tours with an interpreter of Portuguese Sign Language and International Sign Language, as well as sensorial experiences.

SINTRA'S MONUMENTS
& Architectural Treasures

01 Palácio Nacional da Pena

The most emblematic monument in Sintra; an outstanding example of 19th-century Portuguese Romanticism.

02 Quinta da Regaleira

One of the most enigmatic places in Sintra. The architecture and landscape have the signature of Luigi Manini, emphasising the Neo-Manueline and Renaissance styles.

03 Palácio Nacional de Sintra

For almost eight centuries, this palace served as a residence for the Portuguese monarchy and court.

04 Palácio Nacional de Queluz

Constructed in the 18th century as a summer palace, it was home to two generations of monarchs. It stands out for its opulent rooms and lush gardens.

05 Castelo dos Mouros

Built between the 8th and 9th centuries, this is a remarkable Islamic testament in the region. The top of the castle offers one of the best views over Sintra.

06 Convento dos Capuchos

Also known as the 'Cork Convent'. With simple features, it is surrounded by dense vegetation.

07 Villa Sassetti

The construction takes inspiration from the Lombard castles that originated in northern Italy.

08 Palácio de Monserrate

With exotic and vegetal motifs, the interior decoration of this palace blends in with the natural park that surrounds it.

09 Chalet da Condessa d'Elba

Built in the 19th century, following the model of alpine chalets. The chalet's garden has botanical varieties from all over the world.

10 Explore SETÚBAL

NATURAL PARK | WINE | BEACHES

Setúbal is one of Portugal's main ports, and its seaside location makes it a jumping-off point for a boat trip to the Tróia Peninsula and its crystal-clear beaches, as well as to the mountains of the Serra da Arrábida and the area's famous wines. Setúbal also boasts the best fried cuttlefish in the country.

MAGDALENA PALUCHOWSKA/SHUTTERSTOCK ©

How to

Getting here Trains leave from the Roma/Areeiro station in Lisbon. Alternatively, commuter ferries link Lisbon and Barreiro, from where it's a short train ride to Setúbal.

Getting around If you're hitting some of the more remote beaches or the Serra da Arrábida, consider renting a car.

When to go The best time is mid-season; avoid the weekends. The area's beaches fill up and roads become congested in the warm months.

GI CRISTOVAO PHOTOGRAPHY/SHUTTERSTOCK ©

Setúbal's Flavours

Setúbal's main market, **Mercado do Livramento** (open from Tuesday to Sunday) is hands-down one of Portugal's finest intersections of culinary commerce. The vast 1930s market hall has a bit of everything, from exquisite fruit to the peninsula's famous sheep's milk cheese, but as Setúbal is a port city, it's perhaps not a surprise that seafood takes up nearly half of its space, and the catch of the day can range from swordfish the size of a VW bug to squid the size of your pinky. Near the market, restaurants serve Setúbal's signature dish of *choco frito* (battered and deep-fried cuttlefish).

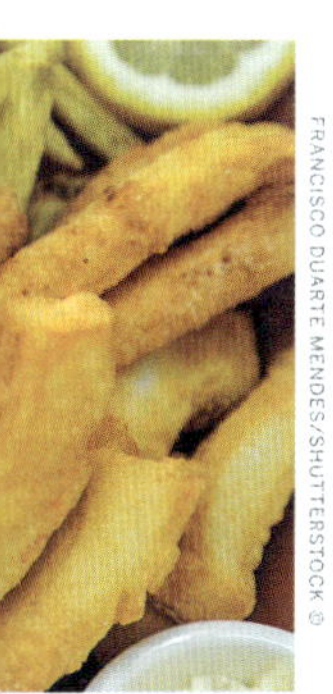

FRANCISCO DUARTE MENDES/SHUTTERSTOCK ©

A visit to Setúbal should involve a stop at one of the area's wineries, such as **José Maria da Fonseca** or **Quinta de Alcube**,

Top left Quinta de Alcube **Top right** Parque Natural da Serra da Arrábida (p95)
Left *Choco frito*

both a 15-minute drive from Setúbal. Don't leave without trying the famous **Moscatel de Setúbal**, a fortified wine with a sweet and fruity flavour.

Museums & History

There are several museums in Setúbal that provide insight into the city's history. The **Museu do Trabalho Michel Giacometti** unfolds in a former cannery, and serves as a link between local ethnography and fishing, as well as the industries that came to supplant them: canneries and lithographies.

From Setúbal's downtown, head to the interior of the Serra da Arrábida to visit the 16th-century convent, **Convento de Nossa Senhora da Arrábida**. The monastery, which was abandoned and closed to the public until the 1990s, is open for visits on Wednesdays, Saturdays and Sundays; call ahead to make an appointment. Nearby, **Forte de Santa Maria da Arrábida** houses an oceanographic museum.

The Setúbal Peninsula's Best Wineries

José Maria da Fonseca
One of the oldest wineries in the area, where the big old wooden barrels rest in long aisles to the sound of Gregorian chants. Here you can taste the historic fortified wine of this region: Moscatel.

Quinta de Alcube An incredible winery with Roman remains, including old baths and an underground aqueduct. And yes, you can taste good white and red wines here, along with Azeitão cheese and egg tarts.

Recommended by Madalena Vigidal,
wine-tourism expert
entrevinhas.com

Left José Maria da Fonseca
Below Comporta beach

Beaches & Marine Reserves

The calm, clear sea and fine sand has earned **Praia de Galapinhos** international recognition and made it an unmissable site in the **Parque Natural da Serra da Arrábida**. Other small stretches of sand lie just a short distance away.

Let the ocean continue to dictate your tour and accept the challenge of a stand-up paddleboard (SUP) session at **Portinho da Arrábida**, or try in a diving experience at **Parque Marinho Luiz Saldanha**. This protected marine area stretches from the Rio Sado estuary to the north of Cabo Espichel. From Setúbal, you can also take a boat trip to see the bottlenose dolphins in the estuary.

Getaway Port

From Setúbal, it's a brief ferry ride to the Tróia peninsula and, by extension, the 'it' town of Comporta.

The **Tróia Peninsula**, narrow and slender and pointing towards Lisbon, is home to one of the world's longest beaches, with quiet swim spots protected from the masses by tall dunes, and even some Roman ruins. In October, the area is a migration stop for flamingos.

At its base is **Comporta**. Formerly a village surrounded by scenic rice fields, it's now more of an upscale destination, home to design hotels and chic restaurants.

11 When in ÓBIDOS

HISTORY | CASTLE | FOOD

Some choose to dress up in traditional medieval costumes, and others prefer to stop at every little shop to see the craftwork or taste a glass of *ginjinha* (cherry liqueur). Óbidos is the most famous medieval village in Portugal, and its streets hide centuries of history and activities to discover. From monuments to books, you can spend several days here without ever getting bored.

SCHWARZE NINA/SHUTTERSTOCK ©

How to

Getting here The best way to get to Óbidos is by car. The trip takes one hour from Lisbon, and there's a paid parking lot at the entrance of the village.

When to go Choose weekdays to explore Óbidos, as the village is flooded with visitors on weekends.

Drink Learn about the history of *ginjinha* and surrender to the sweet taste of this decadent liqueur made from sour cherries.

DIMBAR76/SHUTTERSTOCK ©

Left Street performers **Far left top** Street scene **Far left bottom** Ginjinha de Óbidos stall

Hands-on crafts The Óbidos handicraft, known as Verguinha de Óbidos, is one of the town's attractions. At **Oficina do Barro** you can enrol in a workshop to learn the history of these ceramic pieces and how they are produced. In the end, you get to take your *verguinha* back home.

If you are a music fan, you can discover how a musical instrument is built at the **Luthier Workshop**, examine the tools and materials used in the process, and see projects in various stages of completion.

Escape the tower Enter one of the Castelo de Óbidos towers to play an escape game. Here you will be invited to solve mysteries related to facts and curiosities about the village of Óbidos.

Óbidos flavours Besides *ginjinha*, there are other flavours to discover in this medieval town. Try the traditional cake called Ferradura, or delight yourself with local sausages accompanied by freshly baked bread at a picnic on the castle walls, overlooking one of the best views in town. But don't stop there: end the day with an experience of wine and bites on the terrace of **Casa do Arco**.

Festivals in Óbidos

Festival Internacional de Chocolate Held since 2002, between April and May, this festival is dedicated to chocolate lovers. From sculptures to workshops, show cooking and competitions, everything is devoted to this sweet ingredient.

Óbidos Medieval Market Between July and August the town fills up with jugglers, tavern keepers, knights and maidens, among so many other medieval characters. There are also tournaments, music and theatre performances.

Óbidos Christmas Village During December, Christmas magic invades Óbidos. Count on numerous activities and shows and don't miss the traditional Christmas market and, of course, Santa Claus.

ÓBIDOS' Medieval Heritage

01 Capela de São Martinho

Founded in 1331, it is the only religious temple in Óbidos that maintains its medieval appearance.

02 Porta da Vila

This oratory of Nossa Senhora da Piedade, patron saint of Óbidos, is located on a baroque balcony at the main entrance to the village.

03 Praça de Santa Maria

Built between the 14th and 15th centuries, this square is organised in a Renaissance layout.

04 Rua Direita

The route that connects the village entrance to the Paço dos Alcaides. It gained its name in the 14th century.

05

06

07

08

05 Igreja de São Pedro The church still has traces of an old Gothic portal and has a baroque altarpiece from the Joanine period inside.

06 Igreja de São Tiago Constructed in 1186, this church served the Alcaides and the military garrison, and was the Portuguese queens' and court chapel.

07 Castelo de Óbidos & Paço dos Alcaides The town's most emblematic monument and its palace underwent several expansions between the 13th and 16th centuries.

08 Igreja de São João Baptista Built by Queen Saint Elizabeth's order, this church served as a leprosy hospital in the late 13th and early 14th centuries.

12 The Natural Treasures of BERLENGAS

NATURE | DIVING | WALKING

A paradise for birds and all nature lovers, the Berlengas Archipelago leaves no visitor indifferent. From walks leading to an ancient fortress, to the impressive caves and the fascination of the underwater world, the Berlengas emerge as a natural paradise that you will not want to miss.

MIGUEL PERFECTTI/SHUTTERSTOCK ©

How to

Getting here To get to Berlenga Grande, a boat leaves from the Peniche harbour daily between May and September. Once on the island, all routes are traversed on foot.

When to go The crossings to the island take place during the high season. In low season, you'll have to book a private boat. Choose days with less swell to avoid getting seasick.

Around the island Take a boat trip to see the caves and enjoy fishing or diving.

NATALIA MYLOVA/SHUTTERSTOCK ©

Left Praia do Carreiro do Mosteiro, Berlenga Grande **Far left top** Cliffs and caves, Berlengas Archipelago **Far left bottom** Farol do Duque de Bragança

Getting to know the archipelago The Berlengas Archipelago, located 8km to 11km from Peniche, is made up of a group of islands and coastal reefs: Berlenga Grande, the Estelas and the Farilhões-Forcadas.

The biological richness of this place and its state of conservation earned this nature reserve the classification of World Biosphere Reserve by UNESCO in 2011, including the emerged area and the marine surroundings. This unique ecosystem stands out for its endemic plants and is a protected habitat sought after by several species of seabirds for nesting.

Island's trails Berlenga Grande is the most visited island, and, in case you want to spend the night, there's a camping area (contact Posto de Turismo de Peniche to know how to reserve the tent space). Disembark at the small dock, next to the Bairro dos Pescadores 'Comandante Andrade e Silva'. It is also here that you have a stretch of sand to spread your towel and go for a dip.

Follow the walking paths around the island that lead to the **Farol do Duque de Bragança**, and the **Forte São João Baptista**, the most iconic structure on the island.

Visit the caves Book a boat and set off to discover Berlengas' geological formations. There are several caves and paths between the rocks to explore. If you are a fan of diving, be sure to do it here. The transparency of the waters and the incredible underwater life make this place unique.

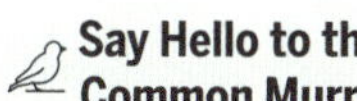

Say Hello to the Common Murre

The common murre *(Uria aalge)* is a seabird that spends most of the year at sea and can be seen between Iceland and Portugal. It heads for land, namely to the cliff areas, for its mating season in the wintertime.

The common murre used to breed in large numbers on Berlenga Grande and the bird is therefore the symbol of this nature reserve.

Unfortunately, since 1939, when there were an estimated 6000 pairs, there has been a decline in the presence of this species in the Berlengas, and they are now almost extinct in the archipelago.

Listings

BEST OF THE REST

 **Family Fun**

Dino Parque Lourinhã

For Jurassic fans, this park will delight the whole family. It features 180 full-scale models of dinosaur species in a theme park one hour from Lisbon.

Bacalhôa Buddha Eden

Giant Buddhas, terracotta warriors and pagodas. You will feel like you are walking through Asia in this park near Bombarral. At the end, you can also try one of the region's wines.

Óbidos Escape Tower

Walking around the walls of Óbidos Castle is a fantastic experience, but trying to escape from one of its towers is even better! This one-hour game will test your knowledge and resilience.

Parques de Sintra

Visit Sintra's historic palaces and estates, have a picnic in lush gardens or ride in a carriage paying attention to the botanical species and animals that appear along the way.

International Karting Palmela

For speed lovers, the International Karting Palmela, besides hosting international races, is perfect to try out your skills as a kart driver. You can go for a team or a speed race.

Sesimbra Safari

Wild beaches, natural pools, dinosaur footprints and socialising with locals. A complete safari-like experience to get to know the area of Sesimbra and Cabo Espichel better.

 **Nature Up Close**

Paisagem Protegida da Serra de Montejunto

About one hour from Lisbon, this mountain range is the highest point of the west region and offers the perfect scenery for hiking and mountain biking.

Parque Natural das Serras de Aires e Candeeiros

Walk among lakes and springs, pass by old rural windmills and go underground in the Grutas de Mira de Aire. All within a little more than an hour's drive from the capital.

Mata Rainha D Leonor

The most emblematic forest of Caldas da Rainha offers 17 hectares of paths among leafy trees. Start at the Parque D Carlos I and take the opportunity to visit the Bordalo Pinheiro ceramic factory.

Foz do Arelho Footbridges

An immense view over the Atlantic and the fresh sea breeze guide you on this path that stretches over the cliffs near the village of Foz do Arelho.

Bacalhôa Buddha Eden

Escarpas da Maceira

Walk along the limestone cliffs that follow the Alcabrichel River in the Vimeiro area and step on Porto Novo beach, the same one that British troops landed on during the first Napoleonic invasion in the 19th century.

Cabo Espichel

Follow the paths that stretch along the cliffs of Cape Espichel, near Sesimbra, and take a look at the lighthouse and the Santuário de Nossa Senhora do Cabo Espichel.

Lagoa de Albufeira

The waters of this national ecological reserve are perfect for a session of SUP, kitesurfing or windsurfing. Right next to it, take a dip in the sea.

Cabo Carvoeiro

At the cliffs of Cabo Carvoeiro, in Peniche, discover true geological treasures. Look for the 'cave that blows', an exit in the rock where you can feel the wind caused by the breaking waves.

Praia do Magoito

Framed by imposing cliffs, Praia do Magoito, located south of Ericeira, stands out for its natural beauty and strong waves breaking on a rocky bottom. Ideal for experienced surfers.

Praias da Ursa and Adraga

Hike between Ursa and Adraga beaches for a breathtaking wild landscape. From the top, find Fojo da Adraga, a deep natural hole with a connection to the sea.

Cabo da Roca

A standout among the many hiking trails you can take along the coast, Sintra's Cabo da Roca is a must-see. In what is the western-most point of Europe, visit the 1772 light-house and look for the cross with Camões' words inscribed.

BAISA/SHUTTERSTOCK ©

Praia do Magoito

Lagoa Azul

This beautiful lagoon, a 20-minute drive from Cabo da Roca, is the perfect place for a romantic picnic or nature hike.

 Sweets & Wine

Capinha d'Óbidos €€

Delicious squeezed juices, freshly baked bread with regional chorizo and Ferraduras, the typical cakes of the house. Everything goes into the picnic basket prepared by Capinha d'Óbidos, next to Praça de Santa Maria in Óbidos.

Oppidum €

Learn the secrets of the most famous Ginjinha de Óbidos with a visit to the Oppidum factory, one of the oldest producers of this liquor. In Sobral da Lagoa, 10 minutes from Óbidos.

Adega Cooperativa da Lourinhã €€

From these cellars comes the Aguardente DOC Lourinhã, one of three demarcated brandy regions in Europe. Discover, taste and take back home.

Casa Piriquita €

Since 1862 Sintra's Casa Piriquita has been serving the famous *travesseiros de Sintra*, a cake made of a light puff pastry with an egg and almond cream filling.

Adega Regional de Colares €€

Take a guided tour with a winemaker to get to know one of the oldest cooperative wineries in Portugal. In Colares, 40 minutes from Lisbon.

Adega Viúva Gomes €€

Influenced by the sea and the Serra de Sintra, this winery in Colares invites you to taste its wines' fresh and saline flavours.

Pastelaria Regional do Cego €

Established in 1901, this pastry shop has been passed down from generation to generation. The famous *tortaas de Azeitão* are the flagship of this house in Vila Nogueira de Azeitão, 20 minutes from Setúbal.

Casa Ermelinda Freitas €€

Learn about the production process of one of the best-known wines of the Setúbal Peninsula with a visit to Casa Ermelinda Freitas, near Palmela.

Water Exploration

Feeling Berlenga

From visits to the Berlenga caves to dolphin watching or a diving baptism. The *Feeling Berlenga* boat departs from the Peniche Fishing Port.

Intertidal

Explore Lagoa de Óbidos by kayak on a scientific tour, accompanied by a marine specialist who helps you identify marine organisms, algae and even edible plants.

Dolphin Bay

Setúbal's bay explored in detail. Choose the one-day programme that includes dolphin watching in the company of marine biologists. You'll tour the main points of interest in Arrábida and stop for a meal and some snorkelling.

Fish & Seafood Lovers

Casa Santiago €

Known as 'the king of fried cuttlefish', this is the perfect place to taste Setúbal's traditional dish. It is usually very crowded, so go early.

Páteo do Petisco €

As the name indicates, this casual restaurant in a suburban corner of Cascais is a great place to dig into *petiscos*, Portuguese-style tapas paired with drinks.

Cais da Praia €€

The fresh seafood that comes out of the Lagoa de Óbidos makes its way directly to the tables here; it also stands out for its cocktail menu.

Tibino €€

With decor based on details and artworks by local artists, try the clams cooked *à bulhão pato* or the fried eels, among other delicacies to die for.

Tasca do Joel €€

A Peniche classic and, for many, the best restaurant in town. The fish and seafood options are abundant here, as are the suggestions on the wine list.

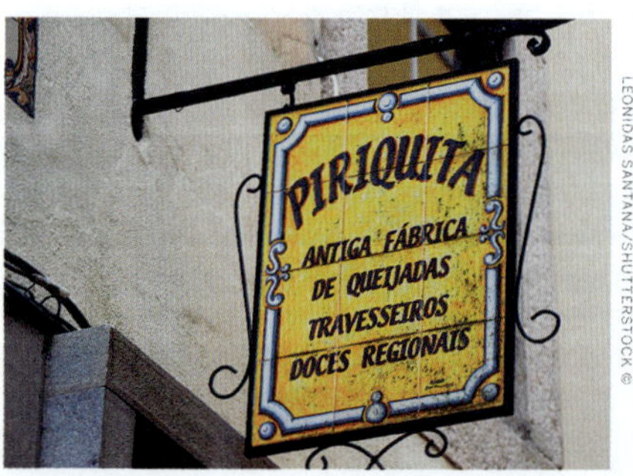

Casa Piriquita (p103)

A Sardinha €€

Come for fresh fish caught off the coast of Peniche, or more traditional dishes such as *caldeirada* (fish stew), seafood *cataplana* or monkfish rice. Five minutes from Forte de Peniche.

Solar dos Amigos €€€

In a small town called Guisado, in the Caldas da Rainha area, this traditional restaurant is known for its generous portions and an enviable showcase of desserts at the end. Try the codfish *tiborna.*

Azenhas do Mar €€€

Dine on lobster, scallops, scarlet shrimps, oysters or a variety of fresh fish, all with one of the best views of the Sintra coast. Enjoy a swim in the natural pool and stay for the sunset.

Scenic Routes

Sintra–Praia das Maçãs Tram

Take the historic tram that connects Sintra to Praia das Maçãs. The 10km route is divided between Sintra's lush landscape and the proximity to the sea.

Cabo da Roca Road

Between Praia do Guincho and Cabo da Roca, the westernmost point of mainland Portugal, stretches a road of twists and turns filled with the beauty of the Parque Natural de Sintra.

Sintra–Praia das Maçãs Tram

History Tracker

Roman Ruins of Tróia

One of the largest fish-salting sites in the Roman Empire and the Western Mediterranean, its ruins can be visited in Tróia, a boat ride away from Setúbal.

Fortaleza de Peniche

This fort gained a reputation in Portugal's democratic history by being turned into a political prison during the fascist regime. Visit the exhibits inside and be impressed by the view from the bastion.

Castelo de Palmela

Climb up to Castelo de Palmela for an incredible view of the Serra da Arrábida, the bay of Setúbal and the vineyards that produce some of Portugal's best wines

13 Seeking Spirituality in THE CENTRO

HISTORY | RELIGION | PILGRIMAGE

Myths, mystery and spirituality define this two-day route through the captivating Centro region. Discover the history of the Knights Templar and Reconquista period in Portugal, marvel at magnificent monasteries, and pray at, or respect, the nation's leading pilgrimage site of Fátima.

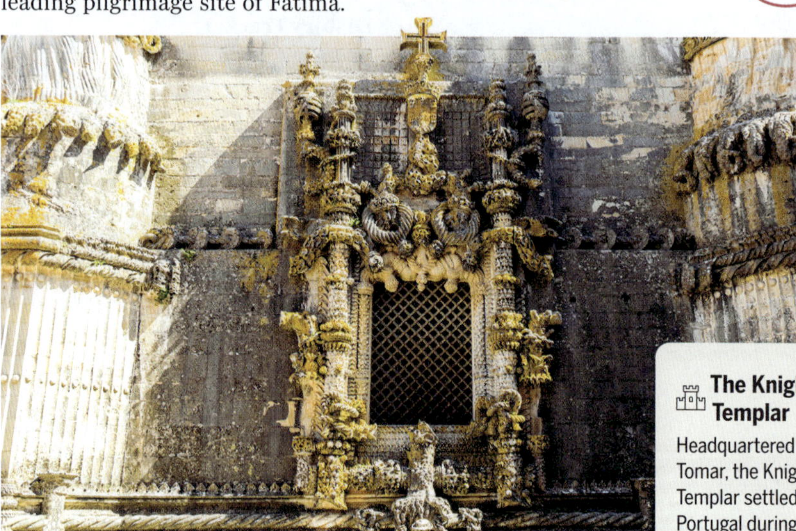

Trip Notes

Getting here Driving will mean a quicker journey. Local buses (rodotejo.pt) and CP trains provide access to most stops.

When to go Major mass celebrations occur in Fátima on 13 May and 13 October. Time travel in Tomar on select dates in July for the Templar Festival.

Extend your trip Visit UNESCO-listed Alcobaça Monastery, or Castelo Branco, where the remains of a Templar castle rise above the city.

The Knights Templar

Headquartered in Tomar, the Knights Templar settled in Portugal during the 12th century, playing a crucial role in the Christian reconquest of the nation. Gualdim Pais, founder of Tomar, oversaw the construction of other castle strongholds, such as Almourol, Monsanto and Pombal.

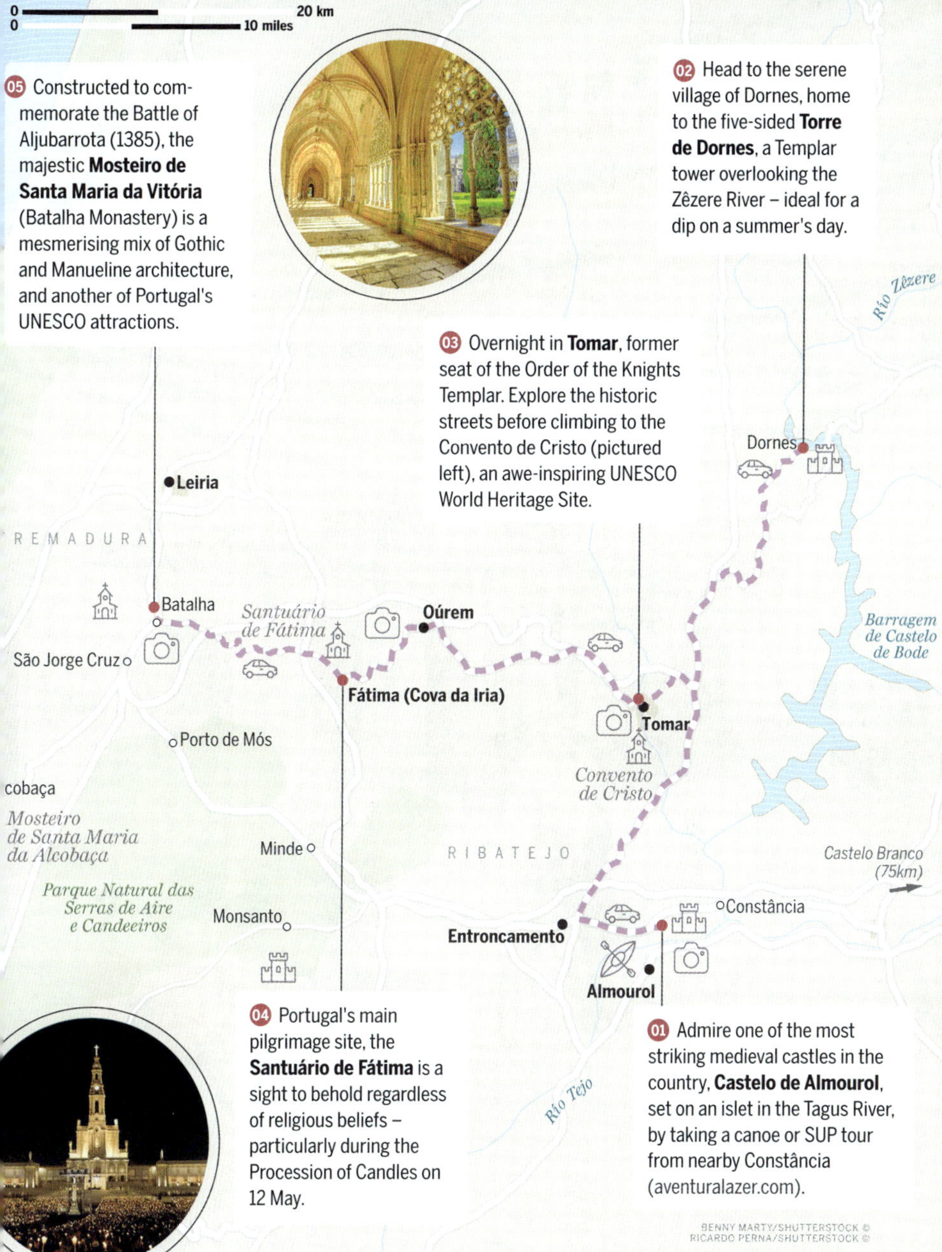

BENNY MARTY/SHUTTERSTOCK ©
RICARDO PERNA/SHUTTERSTOCK ©

ALENTEJO
BEACHES | HISTORY | WINE

ALENTEJO
Trip Builder

Wherever you are – by the seaside, sitting under a tree or standing atop a castle overlooking the mountains with a wine or gin to hand – the Alentejo invites you to slow down and enjoy its diverse scenery.

Explore the ruins and monuments of **Évora**, a World Heritage Site (p118)
1 day

Scale the fortified hilltop town of **Monsaraz** (p113)
1 day

Spend a few days amid the **Alentejo vineyards** (p130)
2–3 days

Visit the pottery workshops in **São Pedro do Corval** (p116)
½ day

Learn how to beekeep at a rural hotel such as **São Lourenço do Barrocal** (p127)
½ day

Surf – or just take in the beach – at **Porto Covo** (p123)
2–3 days

0 40 km
0 20 miles

Estremoz
Serra de Ossa
Lavre
Arraiolos
Vendas Novas
Montemor-o-Novo
Redondo
Évora
Setúbal
Santiago do Escoural
Atlantic Ocean
Comporta
Reguengos de Monsaraz
SPAIN
Barragem do Alqueva
Sines
Santiago do Cacém
Parque Natural do Sudoeste Alentejano e Costa Vicentina

Practicalities

ARRIVING

Lisbon & Faro airports – use Lisbon to reach the coast and Évora; Faro for villages further south.

Évora is home to Alentejo's main train station and bus terminal, offering connections to smaller towns.

FIND YOUR WAY

Local tourist offices provide guides and maps. See rotavicentina.com for details about the coastal trails.

MONEY

Many restaurants offer lunch deals; some only accept cash. Appetisers aren't usually free (and it's fine to turn them down).

WHERE TO STAY

Location	Pros/Cons
Évora	Alentejo's capital city; guesthouses and hotels housed in former convents.
Vila Nova de Milfontes	Country houses, beachside hotels; best for hiking the Rota Vicentina and surfing.
Mértola	Inland, mountaintop village with easy access to both culture and nature.
Monsaraz	Rural estates and stylish guesthouses overlooking vineyards; ideal for stargazing.

GETTING AROUND

Driving is the best way to reach the vineyards and the smallest villages.

Trains connect the Sete Rios station in Lisbon with Alentejo's capital, Évora.

Buses are ideal to reach small cities and towns where the train does not go.

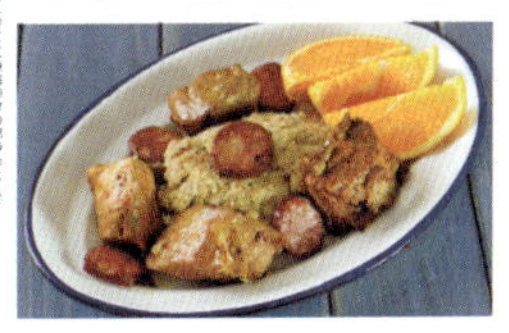

TOP: AS FOOD STUDIO/SHUTTERSTOCK © BOTTOM: NATALIASPB/GETTY IMAGES ©

EATING & DRINKING

Açorda Bread soup topped with poached eggs, garlic, olive oil and coriander or pennyroyal.

Porco preto The Iberian black pig is a quintessential Alentejo ingredient served in a variety of cuts.

Migas Breadcrumbs are mixed with vegetables and/or pork fat to create this filling side dish.

Must-try dessert
Taberna do Adro's *sericaia* (p133)

Best wine experience
Herdade da Malhadinha Nova (p131)

JAN–MAR
Moderate temperatures, perfect for trying hearty Alentejo dishes

APR–JUN
Fine weather and blooming flowers, ideal for hiking

JUL–SEP
Long hot days for swimming and the wine harvest

OCT–DEC
Cooler weather and some rainy days, good for visiting museums

14 The Alentejo's ANCIENT VILLAGES

CASTLES | NATURE | VILLAGES

Whitewashed houses nestled amid the countryside, castles overlooking mountains or river valleys and endless nature trails: Alentejo's byways are worth every detour. Seemingly quiet on the surface, the region's ancient towns have been reinvigorated by a slew of new attractions and diversions.

JOHN COPLAND/SHUTTERSTOCK ©

How to

Getting around Some villages are accessible by bus from Évora or Beja, others are best reached by car. Rede Expressos serves the big cities, while Rodoviária do Alentejo covers smaller areas.

When to go Avoid the scorching sun and make the most of outdoor activities in spring or early autumn.

Follow the train tracks Pedal through old railway tracks connecting the villages of Marvão and Castelo de Vide with Rail Bike Marvão (railbikemarvao.com).

The Roman Influence

Roman ruins are a common sight in the Alentejo. The **Ruínas de São Cucufate** (pictured left), outside the winemaking village of Vidigueira, boasts a partially intact Roman structure thought to date back to the 4th century. **Villa Romana de Pisões**, west of Beja, comprises the ruins of a village dating to the 1st century.

01 In northern Alentejo, close to the Spanish border, **Marvão** stands out with its majestic mountaintop castle that hovers above São Mamede Natural Park.
02 The UNESCO-recognised city of **Elvas** impresses with its star-shaped bulwarks.
The hilltop town of **Monsaraz** considered one of Portugal's ven wonders, and you'll underand why once you step within its lls and take in the views, which tend to neighbouring Spain.
04 Further south, explore the whitewashed streets of **Serpa**, stopping for a tasting at one of the local cheesemongers – the perfect fuel for your climb up to the castle.
05 Traces of Arab occupation have been erased in much of Portugal, but in the hilltop village of **Mértola**, they're still very clear.
Abrantes
Marvão
Portalegre
Parque Natural da Serra de São Mamede
Serra de São Mamede
Arronches
Barragem do Caia
Campo Maior
Mora
Elvas
Badajoz
Vila Viçosa
Río Guadiana
La Albuera
Olivenza
Montemor-o-Novo
Redondo
Terena
Évora
Monsaraz
Reguengos de Monsaraz
Mourão
Villanueva de la Fresno
Portel
Barragem de Alqueva
Oliva de la Frontera
Amareleja
Barragem de Odivelas
PORTUGAL
Moura
Ferreira do Alentejo
Beja
Rio Guadiana
Rosal de la Frontera
Serpa
Sierra Morena
Parque Natural do Vale do Guadiana
São Domingos
Río Odiel
Minas de Riotinto
SPAIN
Valverde del Camino
Mértola
30 km
15 miles
CAVAN-IMAGES/SHUTTERSTOCK ©
BARMALINI/SHUTTERSTOCK ©

15 Crafting a MOVEMENT

ART | CULTURE | TRADITION

Folk-style furniture, hand-woven tapestries and painted ceramics: Alentejo's traditional craftwork trades are kept alive through a circle of artisans who have turned their towns into colourful art hubs. Even the labourers' anthem that once echoed through the fields is now part of this cultural movement. Museums, crafty villages and workshops: here are Alentejo's creative nooks.

LUISPINAPHOTOGRAPHY/SHUTTERSTOCK ©

How to

Getting around It's possible to visit some of the art towns, such as Portalegre and Estremoz, by bus; others are best reached by car or with a guided tour.

When to go Summer is a good time to catch craft fairs and festivals.

Getting crafty Meet local artisans and join traditional craft workshops with the guides of the Portugal Heritage Tours (portugal heritagetours.com).

JOSERPIZARRO/SHUTTERSTOCK ©

Left Traditional ceramics **Far left top** Arraiolos rugs **Far left bottom** Craft store, Estremoz

Art towns & fading crafts The Alentejo is home to the country's largest pottery centre, **São Pedro do Corval**, but other towns like **Viana do Alentejo** and **Nisa** are also ceramic hubs. Nisa is especially famous for its embroidery-like motifs made with quartz, which inspired the redesign of one of its streets in 2021 with red and white cobblestones. In **Estremoz**, the jazzy Bonecos de Estremoz were the first figurines to be recognised as intangible Cultural Heritage of Humanity. Nearby, **Arraiolos** produces intricate rugs with Moorish influences, while in **Portalegre** tapestries reproduce paintings. Further south, in **Monsaraz** and **Mértola**, you'll find hand-woven blankets once used to warm local herders. Other crafts are slowly fading, such as the Pintura Alentejana, a furniture-painting style with floral motifs, and the *chocalhos*, metal bells handcrafted in **Alcáçovas** and used by farmers to distinguish their herds. The lack of artisans in this field has made it an endangered craft.

The music of a revolution When 'Grândola, Vila Morena' was broadcast on Portuguese radio in 1974, it signalled a revolution that ended a dictatorship of nearly 50 years. This song is an ode to the Cante Alentejano, a music genre that has its roots in the Alentejo fields. Once sung by local farmers, this slow-paced a cappella tune can still be heard in small taverns and local associations. It was recognised as a UNESCO Intangible Cultural Heritage of Humanity in 2014.

Workshops & Museums

Olaria Bulhão Purchase hand-painted ceramics or join a workshop at this small atelier in Corval.

Artesanato Zézinha One of the few places still producing the Alentejo-style furniture.

Museu das Tapeçarias de Portalegre Giant tapestries decorate the walls of this fabulous Portalegre museum.

Centro Interpretativo do Tapete de Arraiolos Learn the history of the Arraiolos tapestries and take home a mini rug kit.

Fábrica Alentejana de Lanifícios Colourful handloomed woollen blankets hang within this Monsaraz factory.

Oficina de Tecelagem de Mértola Peek inside this weaving workshop near the church of Mértola.

Irmãs Flores An atelier dedicated to the Bonecos de Estremoz run by a sister-duo.

CRAFTS
of the Alentejo

01 Tapetes de Arraiolos
Embroidery wool rugs produced in Arraiolos, a tradition inherited by the Moors who settled here around the 16th century.

02 Pintura Alentejana
Red, blue and green are the traditional colours used in this painted furniture style famous for its floral motifs.

03 Cante Alentejano
For special performances of Cante Alentejano, singers put on a traditional attire that includes a hat, vest and scarf.

04 Capote Alentejano
Wool cloak with a fur collar, usually made out of fox or sheepskin. These heavy cloaks were once used to warm the local shepherds.

05 Cork Products
The Alentejo is renowned for its cork. Some of it is used to produce fashion items such as bags, hats, shoes and wallets.

06 Chocalhos

For more than 2000 years, the clang of these metal rattles was a common sound in the Alentejo. but now they're slowly disappearing.

07 Bonecos de Estremoz

Colourful handcrafted clay figures produced in Estremoz. Saints are common motifs, as well as the *primaveras* (women with flowers around their heads).

08 Tapeçarias de Portalegre

Paintings can be replicated into stunning hand-woven pieces thanks to the intricate stitch used in the Portalegre-style tapestries.

09 Olaria Pedrada de Nisa

In Nisa, ceramicists are known as *bordadeiras de pedra* (stone embroiderers) as they use pieces of quartz to adorn the clay.

16 Past & Present in ÉVORA

DAY TRIP | HISTORY | RUINS

A time capsule of Portugal's past, the city of Évora has earned its World Heritage status. Here, Neolithic monuments stand alongside Roman ruins and Gothic churches embellished with blue-and-white tiles. As the capital of the Alentejo, Évora is the perfect starting point for a tour of the region.

ANDRES NAGA/SHUTTERSTOCK ©

How to

Getting here & around A train from Lisbon to Évora takes about 1½ hours. You can cover most of the attractions on foot, except the megalithic sites, which are best reached with a tour.

When to go Spring and early autumn are the best times to avoid the heat but still enjoy sunny days.

Pastry stop Try traditional conventual sweets, such as *queijadas* or *pão de rala,* at Pastelaria Conventual Pão de Rala.

JOAO MANITA/SHUTTERSTOCK ©

Left Alto de São Bento
Far left top Templo Romano, Évora
Far left bottom Ecopista de Évora

Find Your Route

Prehistory Évora's early origins can be traced to **Alto de São Bento**, once one of the largest prehistoric villages in the region, and now a favourite spot for sunsets. The **Centro Interpretativo dos Almendres** hosts prehistoric-themed workshops and is the meeting point for tours of the surrounding menhirs (far older than Stonehenge). Think firing arrows, ceramics and hand-carved stone plaques.

Roman gems Traces of the Romans' presence are still visible in the **Templo Romano** and the thermal baths uncovered beneath the city council. The **Museu Nacional Frei Manuel do Cenáculo** holds many of the relics discovered in the region.

Bones, frescoes & tiles The **Igreja de São Francisco** intrigues visitors with its eerie bone chapel, while the **Convento dos Lóios** stands out with its tile-covered interior. For panoramic views of the city, make sure to climb up to the cathedral's terrace. Since you're nearby, don't miss the animal frescoes hidden within the **Centro de Arte e Cultura Eugénio de Almeida**.

Fly, hike or cycle Jump out of a plane and glide above the Alentejo clouds with a skydiving experience offered at the **Aeródromo Municipal de Évora** or ride a hot-air balloon and enjoy incredible views over the meadows and church spires. Rather keep your feet on the ground? You can follow a section of the **Santiago pilgrimage route** (caminhosdesantiago alentejoribatejo.pt) or cycle along the **Ecopista de Évora**, stopping for a glass of wine at the **Fitapreta vineyard**.

Megalithic Évora

The confluence of the rivers Tejo, Sado and Guadiana and the abundance of granite outcrops made Évora an ideal settlement for the Neolithic people. These communities were the first *alentejanos*, the ones that cultivated the land and domesticated the animals, a tradition that is still alive today through the region's shepherds. Of the remaining Neolithic sites, the Cromeleque dos Almendres stands out as one of the largest megalithic settlements in Europe, but the Anta Grande do Zambujeiro and the Gruta do Escoural are also worth visiting.

Mário Carvalho, archaeologist at Ebora Megalithica *@ebora_megalithica*

A Journey Through Time

LAYERS OF PORTUGAL'S PAST UNFOLD IN ÉVORA

Since becoming a UNESCO Heritage Site, Alentejo's sleepy capital has gained global recognition. But Roman emperors and Portuguese kings saw Évora's appeal centuries ago when they settled here. From royal getaway to the rise of the Inquisition, here's how Évora has switched roles through the years.

Left Praça do Giraldo **Centre** Évora street scene **Right** Palácio de Dom Manuel

SAIKO3P/SHUTTERSTOCK ©

Every city has a meeting point. In Évora, all streets lead to Praça do Giraldo. Under the square's arcades, shops and cafes draw locals, while travellers take turns capturing the surrounding neoclassical buildings. Many forget that this was also the birthplace of the Portuguese Inquisition, a dark chapter recalled only by a victim's memorial, placed here in 2016. Following the pope's approval, in the 16th century, crowds gathered in Praça do Giraldo for the so-called autos-da-fé, a public penance ritual that started in Évora and soon took the country by storm.

Long before the royal family and the Inquisition landed in Évora, the city was occupied by the Romans, who nicknamed it Ebora Liberalitas Julia. While many buildings were destroyed after the country's conversion to Christianity, one managed to survive thanks to its medieval role as the city's butchers. That monument is the infamous Roman temple, Évora's most iconic site and one of the reasons why the city secured its UNESCO Heritage title. The temple was part of a larger forum and was used as a place for animal sacrifices known as the *suovetaurilia*. This wasn't far off from its future position as a butcher's shop, where meat was cut and distributed to the people. The exposed stone columns that you see today were hidden under plaster and it was only in the 19th century that locals realised the value of this building and took the walls down. Traces of the Romans are also visible in the city's ancient arches and in the latest discovery of the thermal baths underneath the town hall in 1987.

By the 15th century, Évora had become a favourite getaway for the Portuguese royal family. Kings and queens built their palaces here and other noble families followed

KERRY MURRAY/LONELY PLANET ©

FULCANELLI/SHUTTERSTOCK ©

suit. In Palácio de Dom Manuel, royal babies were born, while theatrical performances took over the stage. Among the last performances enacted here was a piece by the Portuguese poet Gil Vicente. *Villancicos* were also common, and a compilation of these polyphonic tunes was launched in 2014 by the musical group A Corte Musical. As for the palace, like many others in Évora, it's being converted into an exhibition space.

> Long before the royal family and the Inquisition landed in Évora, the city was occupied by the Romans, who nicknamed it Ebora Liberalitas Julia.

Not long after the royal family's arrival, Évora established its university in 1559, the second oldest in Portugal, followed by Coimbra. Originally run by the Jesuits, it was sadly targeted by Marquês de Pombal (1699–1782), who ordered the school's closing in 1779 following a period of Jesuit oppression, which swept across Europe in the Age of Enlightenment. Teachers were sent into exile or incarcerated, and the doors were closed for nearly two centuries. It was only in 1973 that it reopened, giving the young population of the Alentejo a chance to sign up to university without moving too far from home. Today, these students are the living soul of Évora.

A Roman Bath

If you've ever wanted to experience a Roman thermal bath, head to the **In Acqua Veritas Spa** (inacquaveritas.com) just a few steps off Praça do Giraldo. This spa tries to recreate the Roman baths' setting and is the only one of its kind in Portugal. Like the ancient baths, this one consists of three pools at different temperatures: the *tepidarium* (warm water at around 32°C), the *caldarium* (very hot water around 40°C) and the *frigidarium* (cold water around 16°C). It's also possible to book massages or enjoy tea and wine in their winter garden.

17 At the BEACH

BEACHES | HIKING | SURFING

Horse riding along the sand, surfing at a secluded beach or hiking one of Portugal's best coastal trails: visitors can find it all amid the sea and the river dams scattered across the Alentejo.

ALEXANDER SPATARI/GETTY IMAGES ©

How to

Getting here Coastal towns like Vila Nova de Milfontes and Sines are accessible by bus from Lisbon or the Algarve; other areas are best reached by car.

When to go Weather is best in late spring and summer, but visiting off-season means you'll often have the beach to yourself.

Island trip Hop on a boat and go snorkelling off Ilha do Pessegueiro, a small island off the coast of Porto Covo. Trips only available in the summer.

OLGA KOBERIDZE/SHUTTERSTOCK ©

Beaches

By the sea A string of wild and secluded beaches surround the coast of the Alentejo. Here, it's still possible to find an empty patch of sand even in the height of summer. **Praia da Comporta** and the **Tróia Peninsula** are technically part of the Alentejo, but are easily accessed via Lisbon (p95). Don't miss a visit to the nearby **Cais Palafítico da Carrasqueira**, a fishers' port carefully balanced on stilts.

Head to **Porto Covo** or **Sines** for the best wave action or paddle your way to the beaches of **Vila Nova de Milfontes**. People with disabilities can also experience the waves with the help of the SURFaddict Association (surfadaptado.pt).

At **Praia da Samoqueira**, picturesque natural pools emerge at low tide, and further south

JULIAN GAZZARD/SHUTTERSTOCK ©

Midsummer Party

Music festivals liven up the Alentejo coast around July and August. Dance to world music at the **Festival Músicas do Mundo** in Sines or head to Zambujeira do Mar for **MEO Sudoeste** and enjoy a swim in the canal between sets.

Left Cais Palafítico da Carrasqueira **Above left** Praia do Malhão, Vila Nova de Milfontes **Above right** Ilha do Pessegueiro

the **Praia do Cavaleiro** is one of the region's smallest coves, near Cape Sardão, the perfect sunset spot.

Rivers & dams The region's rivers and dams have created many inland beaches. There's **Praia Fluvial do Gameiro** with its riverside walkway and the idyllic waters of **Pego das Pias** near Odemira. It's around here that you'll find the **Santa Clara Dam**, a great fishing site.

Near the Spanish border, you can join a boat trip across the **Alqueva Dam** or relax at the **Praia Fluvial de Monsaraz**, which features both sand and grassy areas, as well as wheelchair access. In Mértola, within the Guadiana Natural Park is the **Albufeira da Tapada Grande**, close to the now-abandoned mining site of São Domingos.

Alentejo's Best Surfing Spots

L-Point, Porto Covo
Portugal's most fun wave, ideal for goofy foots. Three sections with room for creativity, where it's still possible to surf alone sometimes.

Lagoa de Santo André
A concealed wave, which is either epic or so bad you can't surf. You need to combine the winds and swell with the perfect opening of the lagoon to the sea, and then the tubes will come.

Pico Louco, São Torpes
One of Alentejo's most popular waves. Versatile peak, with easy but powerful rights and lefts, rolling over a partially sand-covered rock shelf.

■ **Recommended by João Kopke**, professional surfer @joaokopke

Left Lagoa de Santo André
Below Zambujeira do Mar

Coastal Trails & Villages

Nature lovers will enjoy hiking or cycling across the region's natural reserves. The **Sado Estuary**, accessible from Lisbon (p95), is the ideal place to spot dolphins and flamingos, but the area's biggest draw is the **Costa Vicentina** (p134), a coastal park that stretches all the way to the Algarve.

The Alentejo coast is home to charming villages such as **Zambujeira do Mar**. Arrive early in the morning and head to **Entrada da Barca** to see the fishers returning with their catch on colourful wooden boats. A bit further inland, the **Aldeia de Santa Susana** and **Santa-Clara-a-Velha** stand out with their clusters of iconic houses framed in white and blue.

18 A House in the COUNTRY

NATURE | ACTIVITIES | AGRICULTURE

Not content to simply recline during your time in the Alentejo? Consider a stay at one of the region's *agroturismos*: accommodation that offers guests the chance to partake in land-based activities such as harvesting olives and grapes, feeding animals, producing cork and keeping bees. Located in rural settings, they're also clever bases from which to explore Portugal's heartland.

INAQUIM/GETTY IMAGES ©

How to

Getting around Renting a car gives you the most freedom to explore rural Alentejo. Car rental is available in Évora, which also serves as a good base for the region.

When to go Align your visit with the autumn months if you'd like to take part in the olive and grape harvests.

Family fun Many of Alentejo's *agroturismos* offer child-friendly, farm-based activities such as feeding animals.

PIXEL TO THE PEOPLE/SHUTTERSTOCK ©

HEADSPINPHOTO/SHUTTERSTOCK ©

Left Olive grove
Far left top Vineyards, Alentejo
Far left bottom Cork oak tree

São Lourenço do Barrocal, located near Reguengos de Monsaraz in the eastern Alentejo, offers a host of farm-centred activities, ranging from beekeeping to yarn production. You can also take in the surrounding countryside via horse riding and birdwatching.

A Casa do Governador, just outside Évora, is linked to an active vineyard that has been owned by the same family for a century, so take a carriage ride around the grounds to visit thousand-year-old olive trees. Help harvest fruit and vegetables at the 100-hectare farm at **Cucumbi**, a small resort located west of of Évora. When done, enjoy the fruits of your labour via a meal at the resort's vegetarian restaurant. A yoga studio and ceramics workshop provide additional active pursuits. And set in 400 hectares of cork groves northwest of Évora is **Herdade No Tempo**. The stylish home is on the grounds of an active farm, complete with gardens, goats, sheep and horses.

Herdade dos Grous, an estate located south of Beja, produces lauded wine and olive oil, and is located on a working farm with livestock. **Herdade da Malhadinha Nova**, also south of Beja, offers a host of agricultural activities designed especially for kids. A vineyard and stud farm provide distractions for adults.

Farm Stays

Looking for something more substantial than a brief *agroturismo* stay? Then consider a stint working on a farm in Alentejo. Websites such as **Portugal Farm Experiences** (portugalfarmexperience.com), **Workaway** (workaway.info) and **Worldwide Opportunities on Organic Farms** (WWOOF; wwoof.pt/en/) provide frequently updated volunteer opportunities. A typical experience provides food and accommodation in exchange for a half-day's work. The requirements can differ with each particular experience, some of which require minimum stays that can span multiple weeks; be sure to read the fine print.

The Alentejo's Cured Hams

THE ALENTEJO'S OAK FORESTS ARE THE SOURCE OF THE FINEST CURED HAMS

Many of us are familiar with Spanish *jamón* or Italian prosciutto, but the Alentejo is home to a pork product that deserves the same level of recognition: *presunto*. This is Portugal's take on cured ham, and it gets its distinctive flavour from a unique breed of pigs on a special diet.

Right Dry-cured ham **Centre** Cork oak grove **Right** *Presunto*

The History

Nobody knows exactly when we started preserving pork, but drawings and sculptures show that humans have been encountering pigs in the Iberian Peninsula since the Neolithic area, as far back as 1000 BCE.

The Raw Materials

There is a wide variety of cured hams in Portugal, but arguably the most prized is that made from the rear legs of *porco preto* (Iberian black pigs) and *porco alentejano* (Alentejo pigs). The best pigs are reared mainly in the open in the oak foreasts of the eastern Alentejo, and fed on a diet of acorns. Their unique diet gives the meat a red hue with lots of marbling, or fat, as well as a wonderfully nutty flavour. A rarely acknowledged fact is that the pigs for Spain's most cherished *jamón* are raised among the oak trees of Portugal before being shifted across the border for processing.

The Process

Barrancos, which is located near the border with Spain, is the origin of some of the Alentejo's most prized *presunto*. In Barrancos, *presunto* is made from pigs born between October and December. The pigs are slaughtered when they're between 12 and 24 months old.

The haunches (ham) of the pigs are rinsed with wine and buried in coarse salt. They are cured in this salt for as long as two weeks. The salt is rinsed off, and the hams are hung to dry for a few days. They are then moved to hang in temperature- and moisture-controlled rooms for around

PIXEL TO THE PEOPLE/SHUTTERSTOCK ©

MAURO RODRIGUES/SHUTTERSTOCK ©

a month. During this time, the salt continues to do its job, preventing the meat from spoiling while also extracting any water that is present, thus leaving the meat dense and concentrated.

From here, the hams are hung in rooms that are exposed to warm outside air for a minimum of six months. This stage encourages 'sweating', which causes the fat and the meat to mix. Finally, the hams are shifted to cellars where they will cure for as long as three years (and sometimes even longer). At the end of this process, the hams will have lost between 30% and 40% of their initial weight, but the meat will boast a deep ruby hue, a fine texture, and plenty of complex flavours and aromas.

To source the highest-quality Alentejo-style *presunto*, look for labels that include the terms *porco preto, porco alentejano* or *belota*, the latter meaning 'acorns'.

Shopping List

To source the highest-quality Alentejo-style *presunto*, look for labels that include the terms *porco preto*, *porco alentejano* or *belota*, the latter meaning 'acorns'. *Presunto* from Barrancos has DOP recognition (Denominação de Origem Protegida; literally 'Protected Designation of Origin'), meaning there are strict rules that define how it's made and the ingredients used to make it – all the ingredients to make the *presunto* must be from Barrancos. *Presunto* brands such as Absoluto and SEL have good reputations.

Tasting Notes

A good *presunto* should tasty meaty and acidic – a type of acidity like olive oil, making it spicy in the throat. It should be salty, but not too much – the salt shouldn't take over. Also, there should be some umami and a ferric taste. *Presunto* should have tiny crystals, like in parmesan; if you find those, you know it's a good one!

The ideal *presunto* described by Miguel Peres, chef and owner of Lisbon nose-to-tail restaurant Pigmeu *@miguelazevedoperes*

19 The Alentejo UNCORKED

WINE | HISTORY | DAY TRIP

While it's hard to pinpoint who brought wine to the party, records show that Phoenicians, Greeks and Romans all drank their share when they landed in the Alentejo. With plenty of sun, light winds and flatlands, this has proven to be the ideal spot for vine-growing. So grab a glass and get ready to experience one of Portugal's best wine regions.

SOPOTNICKI/SHUTTERSTOCK ©

How to

Getting around There are some vineyards near Évora and Beja, but most are located in rural lands on the outskirts. It's best to drive there or arrange a guided tour.

When to go Visit in early summer for a tour in milder temperatures or come around early autumn to catch the *vindimas* (grape harvest). September is the ideal time to join the barefoot stomping.

Stay among the vines Spend the night at the L'and Vineyards and enjoy spa treatments using regional grapes and wines.

RICHARD SEMIK/SHUTTERSTOCK ©

MATT MUNRO/LONELY PLANET ©

Left Alentejo vineyard **Far left top** Adega Mayor **Far left bottom** Alentejo Wine Route

A bittersweet tale Wine production was already here when the Romans settled, but they turned it up a notch. With the arrival of the Moors it was cut short, a dry spell that lasted for centuries. The vineyards flourished again in the 1500s, only to be left behind once more with Marquês de Pombal's leaning towards the Douro region. Doubly so after Salazar's (1889–1970) campaign to turn the Alentejo into the country's breadbasket, uprooting vineyards in favour of grain and wheat. Even with fewer plots, the Alentejo vineyards continued thanks to those small producers who stuck to it, and today almost half of the country's production comes from here.

Know your wine Alentejo's balmy climate is ideal for grape ripening, but the coolness of the mountains brings diversity to its wines. Alentejo is renowned for its reds, full-bodied with black fruit aromas, but there's been a recent move towards whites with smooth tropical hints. The *castas* (grape varieties) are often mixed to create a well-balanced blend. Head towards Campo Maior for a yoga class with wine at the **Adega Mayor** or join a wine course at **Herdade da Malhadinha Nova** near Beja. In Vidigueira, **Honrado Vineyards** produces *vinho de talha*, a wine aged in a ceramic amphora, as the Romans did over 2000 years ago. **Fitapreta**, in Évora, is among the few producing a white version of this wine. It's also around here that you'll find the **Alentejo Wine Route** headquarters (vinhosdoalentejo.pt).

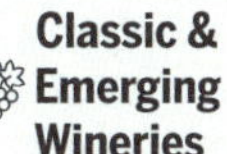

Classic & Emerging Wineries

Herdade do Mouchão A classic for red wines; pairs well with *secretos de porco*, a traditional grilled pork dish.

Quinta do Mouro Another high-rated red, produced in mostly unirrigated schist soils around Estremoz.

Dona Maria Júlio Bastos Traditional foot-treading in marble mills and old *castas* result in potent red wines.

Fitapreta Long-lost grapes such as Tamarez and Alicante-Branco bloom once more at this Évora winery.

Adega do Monte Branco Deep red wines by a fairly recent winery created by Luís Louro.

Susana Esteban Up-and-coming white wines hailing from the mountains of Portalegre.

Recommended by António Maçanita, winemaker at Fitapreta *@fitapreta.vinhos*

Listings

BEST OF THE REST

Nature at its Best

Parque Ecológico do Gameiro

Capped herons and kingfishers often fly through this ecological park in Mora. Follow the Passadiço do Gameiro, a walkway that begins at a small beach and continues along the riverfront, surrounded by wild country fields.

Passadiço do Alamal

About 60km from Portalegre, you'll find this pedestrian trail zigzagging along the Tejo River. Ducks and storks accompany you along the route overlooking the Castle of Belver.

Passadiços da Serra de Ossa

Crossing the valleys of Serra de Ossa, once a refuge for monks, these wooden walkways create a picturesque trail connecting the Aldeia da Serra to a small church on the outskirts of Redondo.

Parque Biológico da Cabeça Gorda

Thematic trails can be found inside this biological park near Beja. Deer are often spotted here as well as *silarcas*, wild mushrooms typical of the Alentejo.

Reserva Natural do Estuário do Sado

Amid the rice paddies of Alcácer do Sal and the dunes of the Tróia beaches is this natural reserve home to dolphins and flamingos. Dolphin-watching trips depart from the Tróia marina.

Reserva Natural das Lagoas de Santo André e da Sancha

Beaches and meadows surround these coastal lagoons where eels and waders are often spotted. Follow the Barbarroxa trail for a hike through the dunes or the Salgueiral da Galiza, a picturesque route through oak trees and willow groves.

Parque Natural do Vale do Guadiana

The Guadiana River flows through this large natural park in the south of the Alentejo. Go for a swim along the margins of Mértola or hike from here to the dramatic waterfall of Pulo do Lobo.

Active Diversions

Coudelaria de Alter

This stud farm near Alter do Chão was created in 1748 to preserve the Lusitano horse breed. Visitors can join tours of the property and book horse-riding lessons.

Amieira Marina

Close to the village of Portel, this marina is the meeting point for sailing and fishing trips across the Alqueva Dam. Sleeping boats are also available.

Cocoon Portugal

Yoga retreats amid the Alentejo countryside are hosted regularly on this farm near Vila Nova de Milfontes.

Passadiço do Alamal

Pork, Seafood & Wine

Páteo Real €€

A native of the Alentejo, chef Filipe Ramalho took over a legacy restaurant in Alter do Chão, retaining the name but adding refined touches to the cuisine of his homeland.

Alento €€

An old primary school turned into a seafood restaurant on the road to Praia das Furnas in Vila Nova de Milfontes, where fresh seafood is made to order and prepared on a wood-burning stove.

Taberna do Adro €

You'll find this cosy restaurant in Vila Fernando, on the outskirts of Elvas. Try the roasted chicken or pork and end with a slice of *sericaia*, a traditional egg pudding topped with plums.

Taberna Típica Quarta-Feira €€

Forget the menu and trust the chef at this family-run tavern in Évora. Black pork is the star of the show, so just pick the wine and let the food parade begin. Bring cash.

Retiro do Ernesto €

From the sausage croquettes to the *caldo de beldroegas* (purslane soup with a poached egg), take your time savouring these local delicacies at this Moura restaurant.

Venda Azul €€

Generous portions and warm service draw visitors to this restaurant in the heart of Estremoz. Order the grilled black pork and don't leave without the courtesy shot of *ginjinha* (cherry liqueur) or *abafado* (fortified wine).

Quinta do Quetzal €€€

Art, wine and food come together at this contemporary restaurant in Vidigueira. Enjoy a plate of slow-roasted lamb overlooking the vineyards.

SERG ZASTAVKIN/SHUTTERSTOCK ©

Parque Natural do Vale do Guadiana

Enoteca Cartuxa €€

Around the corner from Évora's Templo Romano, this bright, modern wine bar serves up quality pours from the well-known Cartuxa vineyard.

Picnic Fare & Handicrafts

Salsicharia Canense

Legendary smokehouse outside of Estremoz; pick up *chouriço* (spicy sausage) and *cabeça de xara*, the Alentejo-style head cheese.

Ar d'Alentejo Wines & Spirits

Wine, gin and liquor bottles cover the walls of this small shop in the village of Monsaraz.

Convento do Espinheiro

Pick up a bottle of oil pressed from the fruit of ancient olive trees at this convent-turned-luxury-hotel.

O Cesto

Inside Évora's old town, on Rua 5 de Outubro, O Cesto sells a variety of handicrafts, such as cork bags, ceramic pots and wicker baskets.

20 Escaping to the COSTA VICENTINA

BEACHES | SURFING | NATURE

Windswept and rugged, the west coast of the Algarve is part of a nature park – the Parque Natural do Sudoeste Alentejano e Costa Vicentina – that links the region with the Alentejo. This refuge of birdwatching, surfing and boundless beaches provides a wild contrast to the resorts on Portugal's south coast, and hikes such as the multi-day Fishermen's Trail provide a unique approach.

How to

Getting here The Rede Expressos bus service will get you to most of the larger towns in this area. The closest train terminal is Lagos.

Getting around The wild nature of the Costa Vicentina means a car is essential to access remote beaches and bays. The adventurous can reach the area via the multi-day Fishermen's Trail.

When to go Avoid the peak summer months of July and August, when the heat and the crowds intensify.

Domestic retreat For several years now, **Odeceixe** – the small town and beautiful beach of the same name – has been a popular getaway for Portuguese tourists.

Inland base Aljezur is one of the more charming towns on the Costa Vicentina, and it makes a good centre for exploring the greater area. Its 10th-century Moorish castle, built over an Iron Age fort, features surprisingly intact walls.

Beach hopping The Costa Vicentina has plenty of near-deserted beaches to dig your feet into: **Praia da Amoreira** reaches inland along the Aljezur river; **Praia de Monte**

Top right Praia de Bordeira
Bottom right Praia da Amoreira

PETR POHUDKA/LONELY PLANET ©

Walking the Costa Vicentina

The 230km Historical Way starts in the Alentejo's Santiago do Cacém and passes through small towns like Porto Covo before terminating in Odeceixe. The Fishermen's Trail, at around 125km, is more demanding. It travels along the coast's windswept cliffs, between Praia de São Torpes, and Lagos. Circular routes allow for shorter walks of half a day or less, so don't let the distance scare you off. Go in spring and autumn to avoid the heat. See rotavicentina.com for more info.

Clérigo is a super scenic spot that's the west coast's most accessible beach thanks to its boardwalk from the road to the sand; **Bordeira** boasts a gorgeous swathe where sand dunes and surfers unite; **Praia da Arrifana** is home to a dramatic backdrop of cliffs and a small surfing scene; and **Praia do Castelejo** is a slice of paradise where the approach along the verdant hill road only adds to the spectacle.

A bit of history The iconic **Fortaleza de Sagres**, built in 1453 and today a UNESCO World Heritage Site, was a jumping-off point for Portuguese explorers, including Vasco da Gama.

FRANZ WALTER/IMAGEBROKER RF/GETTY IMAGES ©

THE ALGARVE

BEACHES | NATURE | SEAFOOD

THE ALGARVE

Trip Builder

Both an adventure playground and relaxing retreat, the Algarve promises coastal escapades, Atlantic swells and epic hiking trails, along with beach bars, islands of golden sands and thermal spa towns. Whitewashed villages, the freshest seafood and local *vinhos* complete the Algarvian experience.

Parque Natural do Vale do Guadiana

SPAIN

Experience traditions, creative workshops, history and heritage in **Loulé** (p157)

½ day

Visit the fort at **Castro Marim**, followed by a natural salt-spa treatment (p163)

½ day

Ameixial

ALGARVE

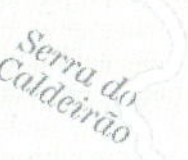

Serra do Caldeirão

Hit the Saturday market at **Mercados de Olhão**, one of the best spots for culinary commerce in Portugal (p161)

½ day

Reserva Natural do Sapal de Castro Marim e Vila Real de Santo António

Barranco do Velho

Castro Marim

Vila Real de Santo António

São Brás de Alportel

Loulé

Tavira

Estói

São João da Venda

Faro

Olhão

Wine, dine and wander the old town, museums and marina of **Faro** (p159)

1 day

Traverse the charming streets, island beach and castle ruins of pretty **Tavira** (p158)

1 day

Parque Natural da Ria Formosa

ATLANTIC OCEAN

Island-hop between sandbars in the wildlife-laden **Ria Formosa** (p160)

1 day

D.BOND/SHUTTERSTOCK ©, AMNAT30/SHUTTERSTOCK ©, JUAMPITER/GETTY IMAGES ©

Practicalities

ARRIVING

Faro Airport Próximo buses connect the airport with Faro's bus and train stations (€2.70, 20 minutes), and EVA Transportes operate a three-times-per-day service to Albufeira, Portimão and Lagos. Visitors staying in resort towns can book group or private transfers in advance.

Coach & Train Lisbon trains connect to Tunes and Faro, where you can join the Algarve line. EVA and Rede Expressos long-distance coaches link the capital to the main Algarve hubs.

HOW MUCH FOR A...

Small beer €1.50

Cataplana for two €45

Parasol lounger rental €10

WHEN TO GO

JAN–MAR
Some seasonal shutdowns and great winter weather for Europe

APR–JUN
Quiet beaches for pre-season dips; wildflowers dot hiking trails

JUL–SEP
Soaring temps, big crowds and peak accommodation prices

OCT–DEC
Good weather, surf and bird-watching – flamingo sightings!

GETTING AROUND

Car hire Allows you the most freedom. Toll roads are easiest paid by an electronic transponder, usually issued with the rental, but can be avoided by using the slightly slower national highway.

Train Comboios de Portugal operates the Algarve train line – tickets and timetables online (cp.pt). Running at a leisurely pace between east and west, popular stops like Faro and Lagos have convenient stations. Other stops, such as Albufeira, are less central.

Buses EVA (eva-bus.com) link main towns, with village schedules designed for commuters – weekends and holidays have minimal services. Local operators provide additional urban services, such as Próximo in Faro.

EATING & DRINKING

Seafood Cuisine in the Algarve is unsurprisingly focused on delicious fresh fish. Mouthwatering local delicacies include *cataplana*, a slow-cooked stew served in a copper pot, usually with *amêijoas* (clams).

Guia piri-piri chicken In the peaceful parish of Guia, known as Portugal's 'Capital of Barbecue Chicken', you'll find the famed hot-sauce marinaded *frango* (chicken) being chargrilled on nearly every corner. Restaurante Ramires is considered the dish's birthplace.

Must-try
Santa Luzia octopus (p153)

Best dish
Cataplana (p153)

CONNECT & FIND YOUR WAY

Wi-fi is complimentary in most cafes, restaurants and hotels, with some towns offering free central hotspots. Data-only SIM cards are affordable and easy to purchase, including from Faro airport.

Navigation Main roads are well signposted – brown signs indicate attractions. Maps don't always highlight trails, but tourism offices supply directions for main routes (cyclingwalkingalgarve.pt).

WHERE TO STAY

The Algarve's accommodation is varied – from luxurious and expensive golf hotels to wallet-friendly all-inclusive resorts, hostels and *turismo rural* stays in the countryside.

Location	Pros/Cons
Faro	Good central connections, varied price points – for most visitors it's more of a gateway than a destination.
Vilamoura	Home to the largest marina in Portugal, with high-end hotels, a casino, premium dining and bars.
Albufeira	Great nightlife, with a party 'strip' and historic old town. Hostels and all-inclusive resorts in abundance.
Lagos	Laid-back by day and lively by night. Accommodation for all budgets and types of traveller.
Monchique	Mountain retreat surrounded by nature, with health-focused resorts and thermal spas.
Costa Vicentina	Boutique rural tourism stays and ocean-side surf school retreats dot the west coast.

VAN LIFE

The Algarve is a fantastic destination to explore by campervan, but illegal camping is a growing issue. Find authorised campsites online at autocaravanalgarve.com.

MONEY

Carry cash – smaller places often don't take cards. *Prato do dia* (dish of the day) and *vinho da casa* (house wine) are usually surprisingly decent and affordable away from the beachfront restaurants.

21 Caves, Bays & BEACHES

BEACHES | WALKS | WATER SPORTS

The deliciously diverse Algarve coastline, where vast swathes of soft golden sands meet dramatic caves and cliff-flanked coves, promises the perfect beach day out. Atlantic swells entice surfers to the west coast, families can unwind on Blue Flag beaches and ocean adventurers will love kayaking into footprint-free bays.

WIESDIE/SHUTTERSTOCK ©

How to

Getting around EVA buses visit most resort towns, and trains serve a few of the principal beaches. Arrive early to guarantee a parking space.

Accessibility The Algarve has 46 accessible beaches with varying facilities, such as access ramps, accessible toilets and amphibious wheelchairs. A full list is available online (visitalgarve.pt).

Stay safe Erosion and currents are a threat. Avoid lounging under hanging rocks, keep away from cliff edges on trails and try to swim at seasonal life-guarded beaches.

LUCYNAKOCH/GETTY IMAGES ©

Pack Your Day Bag

Arm yourself with walking shoes, reef-friendly sunscreen and a sense of adventure to hop between beaches backed by jaw-dropping jagged cliffs, kayak into quieter bays and explore famous sea caves.

Lagos to Ponta da Piedade Towering sandstone cliffs and crystal-clear waters shape this famous point 3km out of town. Dreamy beaches garnish the walk, with **Praia dos Estudantes'** rocky tunnelled archways and the steep-staircase vistas of **Praia do Camilo** standouts. At the headland, descend the steps into a sheltered cove, where fishing boats depart on tours through surrounding caves. Adventurous souls can opt to explore **Ponta da Piedade** on a kayak tour, departing from **Fortaleza de Lagos**.

SAIKO3P/SHUTTERSTOCK ©

Picturesque Pitch Ups

Settle in for the day at these long stretches of sands, with all the usual facilities. **Praia da Rocha** is home to No-SoloÁgua beach club, with striking rock formations to the west. **Falésia**, flanked by copper cliffs, spans 6km from Vilamoura. **Meia Praia** in Lagos offers easy access by train to water sports.

Left Praia da Falésia
Above left Praia da Marinha (p144)
Above right Praia da Rocha

Seven Hanging Valleys Trail Start early at award-winning **Praia da Marinha** before following the signed cliff route to **Benagil**, home to a poster-child cave, best accessed by kayak rental. The trail (6km one way) rises and falls between peaceful coves before officially ending at **Vale de Centeanes**. Continue to **Carvoeiro** (2km); a charming fishing village turned tourism hotspot, for the **Algar Seco** rock formations and plenty of restaurants.

Praia de São Rafael to Galé A mostly well-trodden yet sometimes challenging route (around 6km one way) links bays and beaches to the west of **Albufeira** together, with an occasional detour inland. Join a morning SUP tour of majestic cave tunnels and inaccessible bays (albufeirasurfsup.com) in **São Rafael** before following the tracks and resting your towel on whichever beach takes your fancy. Low tide promises natural swimming pools and reveals access to otherwise unreachable coves.

Coastal Conservation

The Algarve's limestone cliffs have been formed by layers of marine fossils over 24 million years. Erosion has created stacks, arches and hidden caves – where small entrances lead to large grottos, illuminated by sunbeams through blowholes.

Sheltered water bodies, such as the Arade Estuary, act as nurseries to schools of juvenile fish. Swimming and snorkelling, rather than boat trips, minimise interference with ecosystems and allow sightings of colourful octopus, elusive cuttlefish, curious triggerfish and beautiful starfish.

Inês Nunes, a marine biologist who founded Zip&Trip to help travellers responsibly explore Alvor and Ferragudo *zipandtripalgarve.com*

Flip-Flop Friendly

Kick-back and relax on golden sands, coupled with easygoing walks, water sports or boat trips.

Odeceixe Surf the Atlantic and SUP in calm river waters all in one day at this breathtaking beach. **Praia das Adegas**, an adjoining sheltered cove, is an official naturist beach. Take a detour over the Alentejo border for sweeping sea views from the cliff-edge viewpoint.

Praia Grande, Ferragudo This traditional white-washed village retains all its charm, with fishing boats in the seafood-restaurant-lined harbour and a spacious beach under the shadow of an old castle. Take a break from bathing for a responsible marine-biologist-led boat trip to witness wild dolphins (wildwatch.pt).

Ilha de Faro Some of the Algarve's most serene beaches are on the islands in the **Ria Formosa** (p160), with regular public ferries, water taxis and tour boats. Easily accessible by road bridge, residential Ilha do Faro is ideal for a lengthy walk along the sand-dune-backed beach. Continue across the Quinta do Lago Bridge to join the Ludo Trail, a flat walkway with panoramic mountain and island views, plus occasional flamingo sightings. Further east, **Cacela Velha**, with its charming fort village, and **Fuseta**, are magical at low tide when you can wade between sandbars.

Left Benagil **Below** Praia das Adegas

22 Southern ADVENTURES

THRILLS | OUTDOORS | WATER SPORTS

Surf Atlantic waves, cross the coast by bike or marvel at the shoreline – the coastline of the Algarve is undeniably adrenaline-inducing. For those with restless feet, multi-day treks, coasteering adventures and underwater experiences will captivate, while jet-skiing and windsurfing can be found in most resort towns.

SERHIY STAKHNYK/SHUTTERSTOCK ©

How to

Getting around Many activity operators offer hotel pick-up for an additional charge.

When to go Water temperatures peak in August, around 23°C, falling to lows of approximately 15°C in winter. Some activities close in the low season.

Environment & safety Protect the fauna and flora along the coast and stay safe on the cliff-top paths by following trail markers and directions. Always undertake extreme activities with a guide.

SERGE MILES/SHUTTERSTOCK ©

Shoreline Splashing

Surfing The exhilarating Atlantic swell, oceanside retreats and surf schools make the Algarve an excellent address for both experienced surfers and learners. **Praia da Arrifana** is a year-round surf destination, with **Sagres** and **Lagos** both popular surf towns.

Scuba diving The **Ocean Revival Project** (oceanrevival.org), located off the coast of **Portimão**, consists of four Portuguese Navy vessels that have been sunk to create an artificial reef. The remains of a B-24 Liberator Bomber in Faro and wreck-diving in Sagres present even more unique underwater adventures.

Coasteering Experience an adrenaline-packed afternoon of cliff jumping, climbing

PIXEL TO THE PEOPLE/SHUTTERSTOCK ©

The Guadiana River

Voyage inland from **Vila Real de Santo António** along the Spanish border defining **Guadiana**. TransGuardiana tours include a return cruise and time to explore the medieval castle and attractions of **Alcoutim** (transguadiana.com). On land, the multi-day 65km GR15 trail partly follows the river, taking in this history-rich stretch.

Top left Portimão
Top right Monchique (p148)
Left Beach near Sagres

and swimming in sea caves between Sagres and Lagos (coastlinealgarve.com).

Ground-Level Action

Hiking Traverse some of the 300km **Via Algarviana**, a mighty stretch of trails spanning the width of the Algarve. Taking in little-visited villages, lakes, orange groves and both of the region's mountain ranges, the 14 linear sectors serve up something for everyone. One of the most popular day hikes crosses **Fóia**, the highest peak of the Algarve (902m) in **Monchique**, with a challenging secondary trial to the Barbelote Waterfall. For a half-day circular hike, head to **Rocha da Pena**, in the Serra do Caldeirão, a limestone outcrop renowned for birdwatching.

Underground exploring Armed with a hardhat and torch, head more than 200m below at the **Loulé Rock Salt Mine** for a two-hour guided tour7 including ancient geologic formations. Tours depart four times each weekday (techsalt.pt).

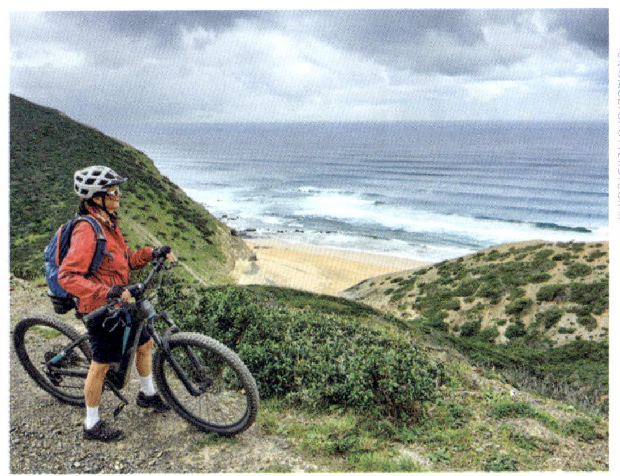

UMOMOS/SHUTTERSTOCK ©

Far left Surfers off the Algarve coast **Left** Cyclist near Sagres **Below** Praia da Arrifana (p147)

Horse riding Equestrians and learners are in good hands at the **Albufeira Riding Centre**, offering one- to three-hour rides on the outskirts of Olhos de Água (albufeiraridingcentre.com).

High ropes & paintball With four locations, including Lagos and Albufeira, climb and swing through the trees at **Parque Aventura**, picking the course difficulty based on your preference, or gather your group together for an afternoon of forest-based paintball escapades (parqueaventura.net).

Adventures on Two Wheels

Not just for ramblers, the mammoth and challenging **Via Algarviana** can be completed in five one-day stages. Cycle through most of the inland Algarve's highlights, ending with a well-earned dip on the beaches of **Sagres**. Details and maps can be found on the trail's website (viaalgarviana.org). For cyclists who prefer a smoother ride, there are numerous road routes to tackle, ranging from flat and friendly to intense. Maps and listings are provided by the Algarve's tourism board (visitalgarve.pt).

From Cabo de São Vicente to Vila Real de Santo António, the 214km **Ecovia** is part of the **EuroVelo** network that stretches from Sagres to Scandinavia. Bike paths and roads link the route, dipping between coastal views and inland towns (cyclingwalkingalgarve.pt).

LEFT: ANA COUTO/SHUTTERSTOCK ©; RIGHT: NIKONKA1/SHUTTERSTOCK ©

23 Inland ESCAPES

HIKING | NATURE | SPAS

Cork-coated hinterlands, charming towns, hot springs and high peaks – the interior Algarve region, mainly around the town of Monchique, is less developed, less visited and longs to be explored. If you're looking for culture, nature and the chance to unwind, but don't wish for a beach or crowds, make Monchique your base in the south.

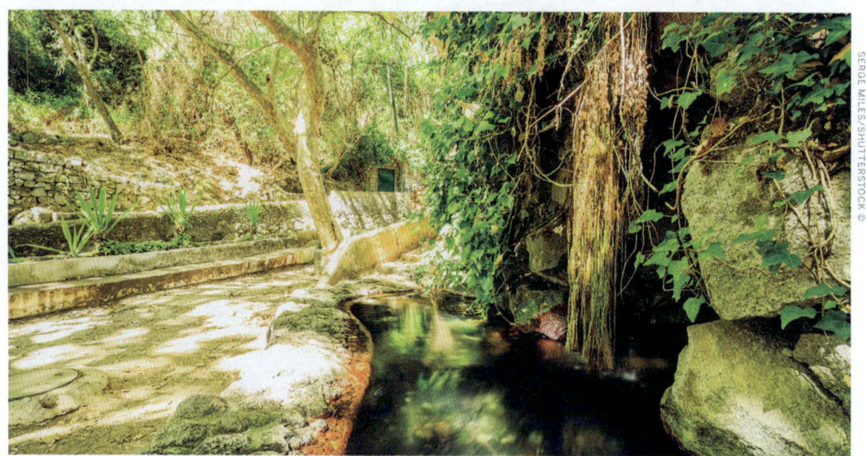

SERGE MILES/SHUTTERSTOCK ©

How to

Getting here If relying on public transport, the only way to reach Monchique (both the town and the hot springs of the same name) is via city bus from Portimão.

Getting around Public transport is limited in the Algarve's interior. Travelling on your own steam, whether it be by bike, on foot or by car, is the way to go.

Birdwatching Serra de Monchique provides sightings of eagles and northern goshawks.

MOUNTAINTREKS/SHUTTERSTOCK ©

Left top Monchique
Left bottom White storks

Healing Waters

Through the mountains of Monchique gush thermal waters that are renowned for their healing powers and high alkaline (9.5pH) levels. From the Romans to royalty, the valley village of Caldas de Monchique has been pampering and soothing visitors for centuries, and it retains a whimsical ambience. A shaded walk through the **Parque Fonte dos Amores**, a park at the northern edge of the village, is the perfect way to cleanse the mind, following the trickling streams as you spot local residents filling up bottles from the source. For the body, book into the **Villa Termal das Caldas de Monchique** spa resort (monchiquetermalresort.com) for a revitalising mud wrap, water ritual and dip in the thermal pools.

Mountaintop Rambles

On the Serra de Monchique, starting at the top isn't a bad idea. From the highest point (902m) at **Fóia**, accessible via car, you can enjoy magnificent vistas across the Algarve and the Atlantic Ocean. It's the starting point for one of the many trails in the mountain range – the **Trilho da Fóia**. The 7km circular trail descends deep into agricultural terraces, through lavender-infused scrub, and along small streams in the cork-strewn countryside before climbing back up to Fóia on the north slope. An alternative loop, the 17km **Percurso Pedestre das Cascatas**, spans three waterfalls and also begins nearby.

The Hamlet of Monchique

Swaddled in the peaks of the Serra de Monchique mountain range, the hamlet of Monchique makes a scenic base for exploring the surrounding area, especially the village of Caldas de Monchique and its decadent spas. The hamlet's narrow alleyways spread out from the 15th-century church, **Igreja Matriz**, and the town also functions as the region's handicraft epicentre. When you're there, don't forget to grab a bottle of the locally produced *medronho*, a delicious spirit distilled from the fruit of the strawberry tree.

24 Taste the SOUTH

SEAFOOD | LOCAL DISHES | MARKETS

Straight-off-the-boat seafood and succulent crustaceans are dished up in *marisqueiras* across the coast. The region's cuisine is defined by fisherfolk – although many shuttle travellers into caves instead these days – and includes grilled plates of sardines and octopus, alongside clams, oysters and cockles. An inland tradition also involves hearty sausages and fig-based desserts.

TRAVELVIEW/SHUTTERSTOCK ©

How to

Market visits Most towns sell fresh fish at their markets. The most impressive is Olhão on Saturdays, when the usual market expands to include additional vendors selling local produce.

Petiscos In October, sample numerous *petiscos* (small plates) and drink pairings from €3 at participating restaurants (facebook.com/rotadopetisco).

Fishy festivals Stalls of delicious seafood spread out across Olhão and Faro, ideal for tasting a bit of everything, on specific dates in July and August.

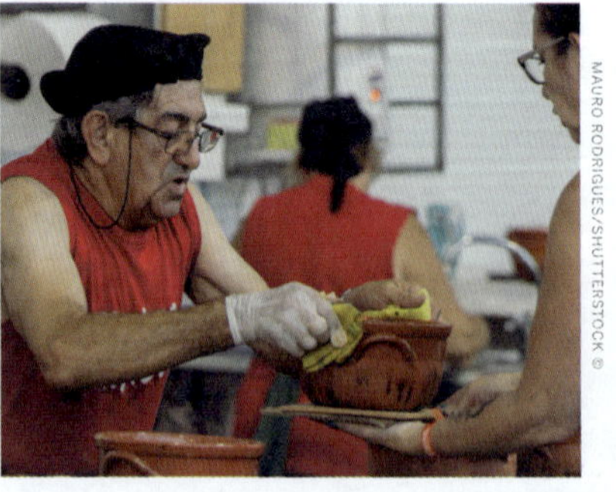

MAURO RODRIGUES/SHUTTERSTOCK ©

TASTYTRAVELS/SHUTTERSTOCK ©

Dishes Worth a Detour

Don't miss out on these Algarvian delicacies.

Polvo The *esplanadas* of Santa Luzia are lined with restaurants all serving one speciality – octopus – and it's here, in the self-billed 'Capital of Octopus', that you'll discover just how exceptional this dish can be. Extensive menus list various preparations of *polvo* – opt for it grilled, baked or boiled to appreciate the fresh flavours.

Sardinha Assada Wafting from the harbour-side BBQs of Portimão, the scent of grilled sardines will tempt you before you even see a restaurant. So celebrated are these salty morsels that the city hosts an annual Sardine Festival for a few days in early August, which has peaked at 100,000 attendees – though you can enjoy this tin-free treat anytime.

Xerém Many locales lay claim to this polenta-like dish of boiled cornmeal, typically supplemented with shellfish.

Muxama Dry-cured tuna loin is sold by several vendors at Olhão's market. Sliced thin, it resembles cured ham.

Farinheira de Milho Monchique's signature sausage combines cornmeal, blood and spices, and comes wrapped in cloth.

Batata Doce Sweet potatoes appear frequently in Algarvian cuisine, with those from Aljezur granted special status.

Figos Across the Algarve, people make a variety of sweets with figs, ranging from dense, cake-like *queijo de figo* (fig cheese) to dried figs stuffed with a mixture of crushed almonds and cinnamon sugar.

Left *Muxama* **Far left top** Loulé market (p158) **Far left bottom** Olhão Seafood Festival (p25)

Cataplana

A **seafood cataplana** for two is an icon of the Algarve's gastronomy. The word *cataplana* itself refers to the clam-shaped metal pan, historically crafted from copper or brass, in which the ingredients are steamed slowly. With similarities to the tajines of Morocco, it's believed to date back to the Moorish period, when the Algarve was known as Al-Andalus.

The dish has many recipes, predominantly seafood-based, with clams or other crustaceans and fish as the stew's core ingredient. Find recipes, or even better, book a Faro **Cataplana Cooking Experience** on the dish's dedicated website (cataplanalgarvia.pt).

THE ALGARVE'S
Traditions & Tastes

01 Cork
Cork harvesting continues in the Algarve. Learn more on a factory tour in São Brás de Alportel (eco-corkfactory.com).

02 Lighthouses
Testament to the nation's maritime history, lighthouses are littered across the coastline, with some open for visitors on Wednesday afternoons.

03 Frango da Guia (piri-piri)
The world-famous Algarvian staple. Chicken, charcoal-grilled, with a spicy chilli marinade or sauce, best experienced at Ramires in Guia.

04 Doce Fino do Algarve
Almonds are abundant in the region, and these colourful marzipan sweet treats are a delicious way to savour them.

05 Medronho
These red fruits distil into *aguardente* (a fire-water spirit). Visit Casa do Medronho in Marmelete (casadomedronho.com) for tours of local producers.

06 Pottery
Colourful ceramics and pottery adorn Algarvian walls and tables. Choose a souvenir and see traditional hand painting

at Porches Pottery (porchespottery.com).

07 Corridinho do Algarve

This regional folk dance, performed in traditional outfitted pairs, sadly can only be spotted at rare festival performances these days.

08 Flor de Sal de Tavira

Used and celebrated in dishes and spa treatments, the *salinas* (salt pans) of Tavira are wonderful to walk through.

09 Wicker Baskets

Basket weaving is an age-old Algarvian tradition. Try palm weaving yourself at the Loulé Criativo workshops (loulecriativo.pt).

10 Oranges

Algarvian citrus fruits are renowned, and the sweet scent lingers inland. Pick up a fresh bag from a roadside stall.

11 Vinhos do Algarve

Taste fantastic wines and visit charming vineyards around the four wine regions of Lagos, Portimão, Lagoa and Tavira.

25 The Towns of THE ALGARVE

CULTURE | HERITAGE | HISTORY

The Algarve's towns and villages reveal their secrets slowly. Narrow streets lead to medieval castles, traditional-craft workshops sit beyond ajar doorways, river sailings link fishing villages to inland towns, and an evening out could mean Michelin dining or late-night hedonism – the choice is all yours.

TRAVELVIEW/SHUTTERSTOCK ©

How to

Getting around Most towns can be reached by EVA bus or train, and are easily explored on foot. A car will make villages more accessible.

Museums & monuments Entry is affordable, often less than a few euros. Hours vary between seasons and weekends; calling ahead to check times is advisable.

Historic stays The Estói Palace, outside Faro, has been renovated as an attractive hotel.

IVARS ANDRUPS/SHUTTERSTOCK ©

Perfect Pairings

Mix and match historic towns and whitewashed villages for a day trip of culture, nature and local experiences.

Ferragudo & Silves Get lost among the bougainvillaea-framed streets of **Ferragudo**, a charming fishing village with a grand beach and seafood-restaurant-lined harbour. Take the train to **Silves**, or if tides allow, book a boat tour up the **Arade River** (ferragudoboattrips.com). Explore the well-preserved **castle** and **cathedral**, and tour the narrow streets of the old Moorish capital. End the day with a tasting at a local vineyard (p165).

Loulé & Alte One of the largest inland towns, **Loulé** is awash with traditional craft workshops (loulecriativo.pt) and impressive historical sights such as the **castle** and

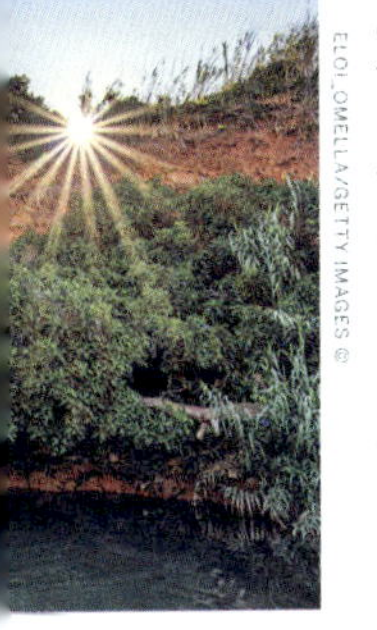

ELOI_OMELLA/GETTY IMAGES ©

Digital Nomads

A small but growing scene, Lagos, with its laid-back coffee culture, is proving a popular destination for extended stays. Loulé and Faro are less touristy and more affordable alternatives – all three have co-working or shared office spaces. Since the pandemic, many hotels have started offering shorter 'workcation' packages.

Left Queda do Vigário (p158)
Above left Ferragudo alleyway
Above right Igreja de Santo António (p159)

convent. Enjoy coffee in the art-deco **Café Calcinha**, and get a picnic lunch at the **art-nouveau market**. Drive 25km to **Alte**, one of the Algarve's most authentic villages, and devour your dishes at the picturesque *fontes* (traditional water sources) before taking a dip in the **Queda do Vigário** waterfall.

Tavira & Cacela Velha The Gilão River, crossable by the **Roman bridge**, links the two sides of this attractive town. Marvel at panoramic views from the castle ruins or **Camera Obscura**, enjoy lunch river-side, or relax on the beach of **Ilha de Tavira**, accessible by boat. To the east, **Cacela Velha** is an enchantingly petite village, with a fort perched above a gorgeous beach. EVA Bus 67 takes 10 minutes, followed by a 1.5km walk to the coast.

A Brief Algarve History

Long before tourists, the Algarve had been settled and redefined through the ages: the Phoenicians first, then the Carthaginians, followed by the Romans – remains of their period are visible in Milreu and Cerro da Vila, Vilamoura.

The Moorish occupation (8th to 13th century) is most evident in the narrow Medina-style streets of Silves, the capital of what was then the Al-Andalus region. Following the Christian reconquest, Jewish quarters grew in Lagos and Faro before the Expulsion, while trade flourished in the Age of Discoveries, both in goods and, horrifically, enslaved people, turning Portugal into a major colonial power. (Lagos was home to the first European market of enslaved people.)

Left Roman Ruins of Milreu
Below Sunshades, Loulé (p157)

Hotspots & Hubs

Faro Stroll the marina, cross the grand Arco da Vila and wander the medieval walled Cidade Velha (old town), where the **Sé** (Cathedral) dominates the square. Elsewhere in the region's capital, museums and side-street cafes will keep you entertained – with the **Igreja de Nossa Senhora do Carmo** bone chapel a unique visit. On Ilha de Faro, the city's beach sits under the flight path. Inland, the **Roman Ruins of Milreu** are worth a detour, while Gusto, one of the region's six Michelin-starred restaurants, can be sampled in nearby **Quinta do Lago**.

Lagos Breathtaking beaches, dramatic rock formations and surf lessons are the main draws to laid-back Lagos. The town centre invites you to explore 16th-century walls, forts and castles. and admire the baroque decoration of **Igreja de Santo António**. Seafood restaurants, cocktail bars and pumping parties will see you into the early hours.

Albufeira Party all night on the bar-clad strip (home to the Algarve's main LGBTIQ+ venue, **Connection Bar**), wine and dine in the modern marina or get a glimpse of the fishing past in the old town. Restaurants, shops and beaches are usually bustling, but you can still get a culture fix at the **Museu de Arte Sacra** or **Museu Municipal de Arqueologia**.

26 A Day Out in NATURE

ISLANDS | WILDLIFE | NATURE

Pristine and protected, the expansive Parque Natural da Ria Formosa stretches some 60km along the coast. A labyrinth of barrier islands, salt pans, wetlands, marshes and dunes, it's a breathtaking destination for wildlife watching, island relaxing, seafood sampling, and nature-laden walks and trails.

Trip Notes

Getting around Tours depart from various coastal towns. Public ferries to the islands are most easily accessed in Olhão; ticket sales open 30 minutes before departure (etrioguadiana.pt).

When to go Ferry timetables run year-round to the inhabited islands, with winter best for birdwatching. The landscape can change drastically at low tide when local fishers hand-harvest clams.

Wildlife Beyond birds, the diverse ecosystem allows for sightings of seahorses, chameleons and the adorable Portuguese water dog.

Overnight on the Islands

Limited accommodation options exist on the islands, including the Orbitur Bungalows on Armona. For a memorable getaway, spend a few summer nights on a private houseboat moored up alongside the islands. Fall asleep to the lapping waves, with a dinghy your gateway to the beach (barcocasa.pt).

05 End your day in nearby **Santa Luzia**, a fishing village famed for its *polvo* (octopus). It's served in various ways at the waterfront restaurants; **Casa do Polvo Tasquinha** is a favourite.

02 Skip the midday sun and head back to peek inside **Mercados de Olhão** before 1pm. Savour the catch of the day from one of the surrounding **seafood restaurants**.

Hire bikes, walk or a tour heading east ugh the **Quinta de im** salt pans for -spotting, or head t for a rejuvenating ting experience in **Salinas do Grelha** inasdogrelha.pt).

04 Drive to the **Praia do Barril** bridge, where a small train connects the island. Sip golden-hour cocktails overlooking the **Cemetery of Anchors**, a testament to the once-thriving tuna industry.

01 From **Olhão**, take the early-morning ferry to the island's beaches. **Armona** is the closest, while **Culatra** and **Farol** are linked by a beautiful beach walk, with kayak rental available.

27 Pamper, Unwind & RELAX

YOGA | SPAS | NATURE

Fresh ocean air, orange-scented lands and over 300 days of sunshine annually make the Algarve an ideal destination for a nature-fuelled wellness break. Pamper yourself with organic salt-spa treatments, unwind in hilltop thermal spa towns or relax at multi-day antigravity yoga retreats. With a plethora of premium spas to choose from, it's simply a question of choosing your treatment.

GLYNSIMAGES2013/SHUTTERSTOCK ©

How to

Spa week Twice annually, for seven days (around March/April and October/November), some of the best spas in the region invite you to experience premium treatments and therapies with discounts of up to 50% (algarve-spa-week.com).

Yoga You'll find drop-in classes in most major destinations, either in resorts or local gyms, though a solo early-morning beach session is equally enjoyable.

Municipal facilities Small selections of free outside workout equipment can often be found in town parks.

STU.DIO/SHUTTERSTOCK ©

SERGIO SERGO/SHUTTERSTOCK ©

Left Spring water, Monchique **Far left top** Caldas de Monchique (p151) **Far left bottom** Salt pans, Castro Marim

Salt treatments Castro Marim, a historic fort and castle village, is renowned for its **Flor de Sal**, and taking a dip at **Salino água mãe** is a memorable way to feel the health benefits. Float in salt pans, soothe your skin with saline clay and exfoliate with salt flower – book ahead for massages. You'll also find similar floating experiences near Olhão.

Thalassotherapy utilises the therapeutic qualities of seawater to relax and re-energise. Enhance your ocean-side holiday at the exclusive **Vilalara Resort** in Porches, one of the most celebrated centres in Europe. Guest spa packages combine both traditional and Thalassotherapy treatments.

Premium spas promise a peaceful escape, and with many in the region offering guest access, you aren't limited to just one. At the boutique **Bela Vista Hotel & Spa** overlooking Praia da Rocha, you'll find a serene relaxation area. A Turkish bath and plunge pool accompany treatments, some inspired by local products, such as almonds. The spa at **VILA VITA Parc Resort** in Porches draws inspiration from the locale, using natural rocks and Algarvian hues in the modern facilities, with holistic and signature treatments.

Retreats are flourishing across the Algarve, with wellness activities built into your stay. **Alamos Retreat** in Guia offers on-site antigravity yoga, **Monchique Resort & Spa** has daily all-inclusive health-focused activities, and **Karuna Retreat** is known for meditation and yoga.

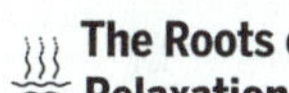

The Roots of Relaxation

A museum rather than a spa, the **Banhos Islâmicos de Loulé** (closed Mondays) opened to the public in early 2022. These are the only (known) example of *hammam* (Moorish baths) in Portugal. The baths, which date to roughly the 12th century, were buried beneath a mansion that was built during the 15th century and the stately home of the Barreto family. The *hammam* were not found until 2006, when archaeologists painstakingly removed several hundred cubic metres of earth to reveal the centuries-old structures beneath.

Listings

BEST OF THE REST

Festivals & Celebrations

Feira Medieval de Silves

Once the capital of the ancient Kingdom of the Algarve, Silves steps back in time for a week in August. Costumes, jousting shows, traditional dishes, flame-throwing and plenty more bring the streets to life. Check dates on the municipal website (cm-silves.pt).

Festival do Contrabando (Smugglers' Festival)

For a few days in March, the town of Alcoutim, on the Guadiana river, celebrates the historic period of smuggling between Portugal and neighbouring Spain. With a floating bridge constructed across the river for the event, you can walk across the water border and savour the celebrations on both sides, with markets, crafts and historical re-enactments.

History & Learning

Mercado de Escravos (Slave Market Museum)

On a dark day in 1444, Lagos opened the first market for the sale of enslaved Africans to Europeans; now, a small museum shares information from this time, although some feel it doesn't go far enough to highlight the suffering or atrocities during this period of Portugal's history.

Centro Histórico Judaico de Faro

The cemetery of the former Jewish community in Faro houses a tiny museum, with furniture and brief history notes of the former Faro synagogue. Found close to the football stadium.

Cerro da Vila

Moments from Vilamoura Marina, this small archaeological site of Roman ruins is the best-maintained in the Algarve. Walk the outside remains, and learn about the region's Roman history in the small exhibition.

Projecto TASA

Keeping ancestral craft techniques alive, TASA (projectotasa.com) in Loulé and Faro has boutique shops of local crafts and occasional workshops to learn skills first-hand.

Family Fun

Aquashow

This large water and theme park promises plenty of entertainment inland from Vilamoura, including a 'water-coaster' and wave pool.

Golfland

The Algarve is renowned for its fantastic golf courses, and this tropical mini-golf in Alvor allows the kids to practise their putting too.

Sand City Lagoa

When sandcastles just aren't cutting it anymore, head to this sand sculpture theme park, just off the EN125 in Lagoa. Designs range from popular music stars to world-famous locations, all crafted from sand and differing from year to year.

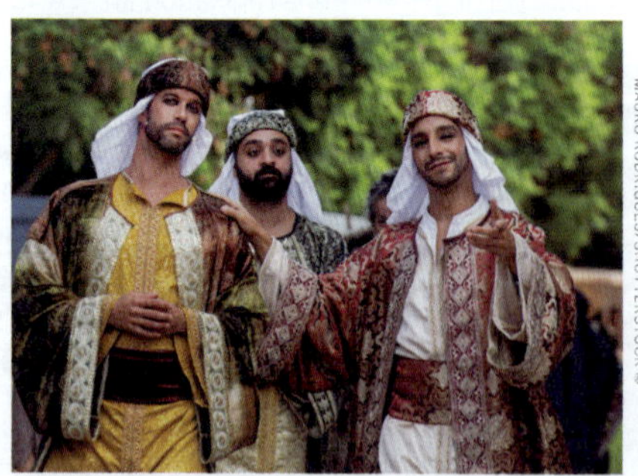

Feira Medieval de Silves

Slide & Splash

One of the best waterparks in Portugal, this well-maintained and large land of slides and pools near Carvoeiro is a fun day out for all ages. Discounts are offered online (slidesplash.com), along with transport options.

 Vines & Brews

Morgado Do Quintão €€

Under the shade of a 2000-year-old tree just outside Silves, this family-run vineyard invites you to lunch at 'The Farmers Table'. Enjoy a selection of delicious local dishes and a flight of wine from the estate. Monday to Saturday with reservations (morgadodoquintao.pt).

Quinta Dos Santos Tap House & Vineyard €€

Find this combined vineyard, craft brewery and trendy restaurant between Carvoeiro and Ferragudo. Taste wines and beers made on-site, alongside homemade dishes. If head brewer Greg is around, ask for a behind the scenes peek into the process (quintadossantos.com).

Algarve Rock Brewery €

Not far from Faro Airport, this modern craft brewery makes the most of local ingredients. Swing by the Tap Room for a tasting, but check opening times in advance.

 Beach Clubs & Bars

NoSoloÁgua Portimão €€

This trendy destination on Praia da Rocha has shoreside loungers, an ocean-facing pool, and musical beats accompanying the extensive cocktail and world-cuisine menu.

Thai Beach Vilamoura €€

Sip on expertly crafted cocktails and devour delicious Thai tasting menus to the backdrop of Praia da Falésia. This bar and lounge is a great lunch spot and equally renowned for its events and parties.

BIGKELLS/SHUTTERSTOCK ©

Vale do Lobo

Caniço €€

Built into the cliffs of Alvor and reached by an elevator in the rocks, this bar and restaurant's cove setting is spectacular. In summer months, late-night parties spill out onto the sand.

18-Hole Golf Courses

Vale do Lobo

With two spectacular 18-hole championship golf courses close to Vilamoura, it's hard not to be distracted by the ocean views at Vale do Lobo, one of the premium golfing destinations in the Algarve.

Penina

On the outskirts of Portimão, the Algarve's first 18-hole course, and home to the Portuguese Open numerous times, the Sir Henry Cotton Championship Course makes for a great round.

Golf Societies

There is a range of Algarve golf societies that allow non-members to play. 6 Golfe, based at Vale de Milho, hosts games across the Algarve, and guests can find and book upcoming rounds online (6golfealgarve.com).

28 The 12 Historic VILLAGES

HISTORY | RUINS | CASTLES

Lose yourself among schist homes hidden by nature, clamber up boulder-topped buildings for impeccable vistas, and marvel at age-old traditions and military forts among the 12 Aldeias Históricas de Portugal, located in the border region with Spain. Take a remote and rewarding journey into Portugal's past.

YURI TURKOV/SHUTTERSTOCK ©

How to

Getting here Car rental provides easy access; however, a mix of bus (Rede Expressos and Transdev) and train journeys can get you to, or at least close to, most villages. Comboios de Portugal offers a summer train/bus day trip to Monsanto.

When to go Spring and autumn have fewer crowds and comfortable hiking temperatures. From June to November, events take place as part of the '12 em Rede' festival.

The great hike For those with plenty of time, the Grand Route 22 links all 12 villages.

VR2000/SHUTTERSTOCK ©

Amazing Aldeias

Make a beeline for these (highly subjective) stars of the show:

Monsanto Mesmerising panoramic views of rocky outcrops, parched pastures and green mountains pierce the sky from Monsanto's prime position high on a hill. Here, boulders and buildings are as one – precariously floating above and between homes while doorways seemingly lead into giant stones. Tight streets of towers and churches, decorated with colourful plant pots, lead up to the Knights Templar castle. By sunset, devoid of day trippers, you'll be left in awe, wondering how this truly mystical place was awarded 'The Most Portuguese Village in Portugal' – when it's as far from typical as you can get!

C-R-V/SHUTTERSTOCK ©

Why These Villages?

Located in the border region with Spain, a few hours' drive from Coimbra, these 12 villages played a crucial role in defending the nation – hence the prevalent fortifications and castles. The Aldeias Históricas programme aims to preserve this heritage.

Learn more and plan your route at aldeiashistoricas deportugal.com.

Left Sortelha (p168) **Above left** Monsanto **Above right** Linhares de Beira (p169)

Piódão Nestled in the lush green landscape of the Serra do Açor (Goshawk Mountains), the schist village of Piódão, unlike the others, is more known for housing fugitives than its role in the country's history. The narrow streets climbing the terrain are a delight to wander. Even more impressive when viewed from afar (especially illuminated at night), the whitewashed and blue-detailed church makes a striking contrast to the stone buildings and surrounding nature.

Sortelha Looking down from the 13th-century castle, Sortelha spills out in all its grand history. Alleyways of granite homes, Gothic gateways, medieval tombs, a Renaissance church and a Manueline pillory combine to tell the history of one of Portugal's oldest towns – all wrapped up in magnificent walls and a landscape dotted with imposing granite boulders (look out for the Old Lady's Head, a huge boulder with an uncanny resemblance to a sharp-chinned witch).

City Stopovers

Accommodation options are available in most villages, making a road trip between them (stopping at two to four per day) an ideal choice – alternatively, the nearby cities can make good pit stops, detours or bases.

Guarda Located centrally to most villages, Guarda is the perfect multi-night base. Admire the cathedral's Gothic and Manueline architecture, stroll through the Old Jewish Quarter, and learn the region's history at Guarda Museum.

Castelo Branco When visiting Monsanto, stopping at Castelo Branco is a must to take in the Templar Castle ruins and views before touring the Baroque Bishop's Palace Gardens – the statued staircases are a spectacle.

The Remaining Nine

Almeida dates back to Roman times and houses military fortifications inside its star-shaped walls.

Belmonte has a synagogue that's a great starting point to learn about the town's Jewish history.

Castelo Mendo comprises two parts: the medieval citadel and the Dionysian walls of the Barbican.

Castelo Novo offers a striking location, set against the Serra da Gardunha mountains, granite houses, Templar fortifications, castles and churches.

Castelo Rodrigo is defined by medieval ruins and sights. The church, cistern and Cristóvão de Moura Palace are of particular interest.

Idanha-a-Velha is easily hiked to from Monsanto. The ancient streets and cathedral of various periods make this Roman sight a worthy visit.

Linhares da Beira is best admired from the skies. Gaze down on the 12th-century village at this popular paragliding spot.

Marialva takes on an almost mythical appearance when the clouds roll in. For a magical experience of the citadel, overnight at Casas do Côro (casasdocoro.pt).

Trancoso, one of the largest villages, is best visited on a Friday for the weekly market – be sure to try the local sardine-shaped fried sweets!

Left Piódão **Below** Linhares da Beira

PORTO
AUTHENTIC | ECLECTIC | HISTORIC

PORTO
Trip Builder

Porto's profile is rising quickly as a prime tourist destination and gateway to the north. The area offers activities for all types of travels, but exploration is best on foot as Portugal's second city is compact and dense with sights.

R da Constituição
R de Latino Coelho
R do Almada
R Sá da Bandeira
ALIADOS
R Dr Magalhães Lemos
R da Restauração
Pç de Lisboa
MIRAGAIA
R de Miragaia
RIBEIRA
Av Dom Afonso Henriques
R Infante Dom Henrique
Rio Douro
0.5 miles
2.5 km

Climb **Torre dos Clérigos** and attend a pipe organ concert (p180)
1-3 hours

Explore one of the city's unique museums such as **Serralves** (p175)
2 hours

Find a shady spot for a picnic with views in the **Jardim das Virtudes** (p187)
2 hours

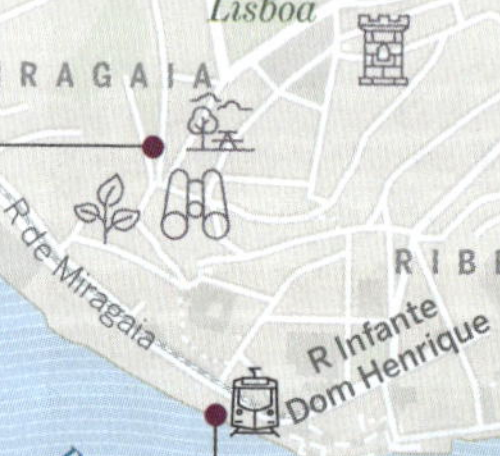

Ride **Tram 1** from Porto to Foz and back (p193)
½ day

Head across to the Gaia port lodges via the **Luís I Bridge** (p190)
½-1 hour

Practicalities

ARRIVING

Porto Airport is 30 minutes from the centre by direct metro.

Campanhã Station for intercity rail and terminus for the *Alfa Pendular.*

Rodoviário (Campo 24 de Agosto) is the main coach terminal.

FIND YOUR WAY

Google Maps and other apps have integrated Porto's metro and bus network, which helps find stops and map out journeys.

MONEY

Look for ATMs with the white-and-blue 'Multibanco' logo for the best exchange rates. Carry cash for small purchases.

WHERE TO STAY

Location	Pros/Cons
Foz & Matosinhos	Hotels and tourist apartments, some with ocean views.
Boavista	Hotel chains in business district.
Cedofeita, Sé, Miragaia, São Nicolau e Vitória, Santo Ildefonso	Boutique hotels offer ambience and proximity to monuments.
Bonfim	Residential but still within walking distance to centre.

GETTING AROUND

Metro covers a large area from Póvoa de Varzim (north) to Vila Nova de Gaia (south).

Buses serve the entire metro area, but navigation can be confusing. Double-decker bus 500 from the bottom of Aliados to the Mercado de Matosinhos is the one to take. Sit on the top deck on the left side for the best views.

EATING & DRINKING

Francesinha, Porto's most indulgent sandwich, with origins from a Portuguese émigré in the 1950s.

Port the city's signature drink – a type of fortified wine.

Must-try
Sandes de pernil com queijo (pork loin sandwich with cheese) at Casa Guedes (p195).

Best bifanas
Pork sandwiches with bite at Conga (pictured bottom left; p195).

JAN–MAR
Mix of rain and sun, may reach freezing overnight

APR–JUN
May be rainy in April, mostly pleasant daytime temps

JUL–SEP
Summer temps 25°C to 30°C; tourist high season

OCT–DEC
Chilly overnight, daytime temps moderate, mix of sun and rain

29 Porto's Quirky MUSEUMS

HISTORY | ART | ARCHITECTURE

If you've reached your limit of ancient churches, then Porto has some alternatives. The city is home to a handful of museums that stray far from from the usual dusty exhibits. They span a repository of the city's unique architecture, a pharmacy frozen in time – in the 19th century, to be exact – and the country's premier photography museum.

GEN_SHTAB/SHUTTERSTOCK ©

How to

When to go Most museums in Portugal are closed on Mondays.

Getting around Most of central Porto's museums can be navigated on foot, but the city's steep hills make walking somewhat challenging.

Pass The Porto Card provides discounts to several museums and attractions, as well as free and unlimited use of public transport. The card can be purchased online before you arrive in Porto. (portocard.city/en).

MARCO MARAVIGLIA/ALAMY STOCK PHOTO ©

JUAN GARCIA HINOJOSA/SHUTTERSTOCK ©

Left World of Wine **Far left top** Museu do Carro Eléctrico **Far left bottom** Banco de Materiais

Banco de Materiais This fascinating repository for old tiles, antique door knockers, ancient street signs and advertisements also functions as a (free) museum.

Museu do Carro Eléctrico Housed in an antiquated switching-house, this museum holds dozens of beautifully restored old trams – from early 1870s' models once pulled by mules to the more streamlined, bumble-bee-yellow 1930s' numbers.

Centro Português de Fotografia This stately yet muscular building once served as a prison and now houses the country's premier photography museum. Walk through the thick iron gates and into the cells to see the exhibits. The unique setting lends intrigue and gravitas.

Museu do Centro Hospitalar do Porto When the 200-year-old Hospital Real de Santo António was renovated in 2013, the authorities decided to retain the stuck-in-time pharmacy, which today functions as a small but fascinating museum dedicated to the history of pharmaceutical science and medicine.

Museu da Marioneta Porto's marionette museum turns the spotlight on the remarkable puppet creations that have taken to the stage at the Teatro Marionetas do Porto over the past 25 years.

World of Wine Set in 55,000 sq metres of restored wine warehouses in Vila Nova de Gaia – just across the Douro River from Porto – this museum features seven spaces dedicated to wine, cork, chocolate, fashion and Porto's history. There's also a wine school, various restaurants and cafes, and a lovely open-air terrace with picturesque views of Porto's bridges and rooftops.

Serralves

This fabulous cultural institution centres around a contemporary art museum and an Art Deco mansion, both of which sit within the marvellous 18-hectare **Parque de Serralves**. Lily ponds, rose gardens, fountains, a farm, a treetop walk and numerous whimsical touches – such as a bright-red sculpture of oversized pruning shears – make for a bucolic outing in the city that's a fun experience for kids as well. The estate is just 6km west of the city centre, accessible via bus 207. Note that admission to the park and museum are charged separately.

By Inês Matos Andrade
Inês is a food writer based in Lisbon. She covers hospitality, restaurants and events.
@inesmatosandrade

Beyond the Francesinha

THE ULTIMATE GUIDE TO PORTO'S BEST BREAD BITES

Amid worldwide accolades for iconic sandwiches like the *bánh mì*, the Reuben and lobster rolls, Porto's heavy *francesinha* - a legendary meat-layered sandwich doused in a tangy hot sauce - stands tall. Yet, tucked between lots more slices of bread lie numerous delectable offerings awaiting discovery.

Left *Cachorrinho*
Centre *Prego* **Right** *Bifana*

STEPH COUVRETTE/SHUTTERSTOCK ©

Not Your Average Hot Dog

Cachorrinho – 'little hot dog' or 'puppy' – differs from what you would get at a baseball game. The *cachorrinho* is a slender baguette filled with fresh sausages and *linguiça* (spiced pork sausage) from Salsicharia Leandro, topped with cheese slices, pressed in a sandwich machine and then brushed with hot sauce. The production process at the original *cachorrinho* house, Gazela (p195), is fast-paced and electrifying, with rows of 30cm baguettes methodically cut for customers to eat. Copycats have sprung up around the city and include The Dog, República dos Cachorros and Alma do Cachorro.

Nail It with a Prego

The *prego* – meaning 'nail' – was created in 1889 at a Sintra beach by Manuel Dias Prego, who prepared thin slices of veal stuffed in an oven-baked loaf. Porto, of course, decided to make it bigger and better. At Offline, the *prego* showcases a pink, tender, juicy and obscenely tall beef loin, topped with cheese, ham and mustard sauce, and served in a crusty toasted bun. Francesinha Café's steak is thinner, layered with ham and cheese, and enclosed on a butter-toasted bun. At Venham Mais 5, the beef loin is covered with buttery sheep's cheese, while at The Dog, the *prego à Hugo* opts for *linguiça* from Salsicharia Leandro, Flamengo cheese and a fried egg.

Ham It Up

Maria de Lurdes was only 17 when she started working at Tasca da Badalhoca – back in 1965 – but she is credited with creating the *sandes de presunto*, a ham sandwich

TASTYTRAVELS/SHUTTERSTOCK ©

STEPH COUVRETTE/SHUTTERSTOCK ©

made with small slices of white bread. The ham shanks are deboned and sliced throughout the day to fill the sandwiches stacked in the shop window, and over 500 are served daily. The scarves of Boavista football club, of which the matriarch is a staunch supporter, share the limelight with the hams.

Football also plays a significant role at Casa Lourot in Batalha, with Futebol Clube do Porto scarves falling from the ceiling. They serve *PO*, or *presunto + ovo* (ham and fried egg). Ham in the north is cold-cured and unsmoked, which makes it more meaty and metallic in flavour, and it's bathed in runny egg yolk.

> At Offline, the *prego* showcases a pink, tender, juicy and obscenely tall beef loin, topped with cheese, ham and mustard sauce, and served in a crusty toasted bun.

More than a Pork Steak

Porto's *bifana* is so much more than just a pork steak: consisting of thinly sliced pieces of pork doused in a spicy marinade with lots of paprika and cumin, the roll is small, slightly crunchy and ideally shaped to be eaten in two bites. In 1976, Conga was the first place to display large pots of the rich, bubbling sauce in its shop windows. Local experts favour Astro, in Campanhã Station, where the meat is still hand-cut, or Sol e Sombra, where it's served with a bottle of extra-hot sauce labelled 'I am brave'. *Sandes de rojão* features pork shanks marinated in a base of wine, garlic and bay leaves; when done well, they fall apart in your mouth. Two excellent places to try them are Casa Expresso, in the heart of Porto, and João da Requieira, an old tavern in Maia, on the outskirts.

Salsicharia Leandro

Salsicharia Leandro is an integral part of Porto's food culture. Owner Vítor Ferreira has operated this century-old butcher's shop in the Bolhão Market for the past 60 years, and it was Salsicharia Leandro that produced the fresh sausages and *linguiça* used in the first *francesinha*. Over time, these two sausages have become essential ingredients in the iconic *francesinha* and *cachorrinho*, and even in some *pregos*. The fresh sausage and *linguiça* are known for their unique blend of spices – including cumin and white pepper – providing a distinctive flavour that true lovers of this Porto delicacy can recognise immediately.

30 Porto's ARCHITECTURE

HISTORIC | MODERN | PRITZKER PRIZES

Porto is an ancient city, its historic centre a living museum of architectural styles from Portuguese Romanesque to contemporary. Across the passages of time, the city was largely spared from the devastating effects of natural disasters and WWII bombs, while centuries of artisans added their distinct layers to its facades.

NIKOLPETR/SHUTTERSTOCK ©

How to

Getting around Porto's historic centre is compact and walkable, if at times quite steep, with daunting staircases. Bring your sturdiest shoes.

Costs There are no fees to enter churches except for São Francisco, now only a museum. There is a small fee for the cloisters and museum of the Sé.

Best timing For the most popular monuments, visit either at opening or closing time to avoid the tourist buses.

FOTOKON/SHUTTERSTOCK ©

IACOMINO FRIMAGES/SHUTTERSTOCK ©

Left Almas Chapel **Far left top** Igreja de São Francisco **Far left bottom** Cedofeita Church

Medieval monuments Most of Porto's preserved monuments from the early Middle Ages lie within the UNESCO-listed historic centre, although each has been restored and adapted multiple times. From the top of the hills down you have the Sé, Medieval Tower and sections of the wall, and the churches of Santa Clara and São Francisco. Cedofeita Church, the oldest in Porto, is outside the UNESCO area and is suggested to be even older than recorded (11th century).

Baroque monuments Italian artist Nicolau Nasoni's baroque style is represented in Porto's most famous landmarks: Clérigos Church and Tower; the Bishop's Palace; Misericórdia Church facade; Freixo Palace; the Carmo Church's stonework and the engravings in Santo Ildefonso Church. His gilt carvings in the churches of Santa Clara and São Francisco, along with Ordem do Terço's exterior, are impressive.

Neoclassical monuments Renewal in the late 18th century led to some of Porto's most majestic buildings: Lapa Church; Carrancas Palace (now the Soares dos Reis Museum); Vitória Church; the Stock Exchange Palace; the Customs House and the neo-Palladian British Association building. During the 18th century, Praça da Ribeira, originating in medieval times, was transformed to its current style.

Tile monuments Porto is famous for its decorative tiles, called *azulejos*, which adorn interiors and exteriors. Large-scale works can be found at: Almas Chapel; São Bento Station; the *Ribeira Negra* mural; the churches of Santo Ildefonso, Carmo and Misericórdia, and outside the Sé.

Porto's Pritzker Prize Winners

The Pritzker Prize, architecture's annual international award to honour significant achievement, has twice been presented to alumni of the University of Porto: Álvaro Siza Vieira in 1992 and Eduardo Souto de Moura in 2011. Both are modernist architects who've gained international recognition for designs that harmonise with natural surroundings. Examples include Siza Viera's natural pools in Leça da Palmeira (1966), filled by ocean tides, and Moura's design of Braga Stadium (2004), melding into an old rock quarry. Álvaro Siza Vieira built the University of Porto's Faculty of Architecture building (1988–1992), integrating it with the cliff.

INSPIRED
by Devotion

01 Capela do Senhor da Pedra (1686)
Hexagonal church built on a rock on the beach, originally a site of ancient pagan worship.

02 Mosteiro da Serra do Pilar (1672)
Circular church and cloister design unique in Portugal; replica of Church of Santa Maria Redonda in Rome.

03 Igreja do Mirante (1877)
The oldest Protestant church in Porto, covered in decorative tiles designed by a church member, Delfim Gonçalves Vieira, in 1934.

04 Igrejas do Carmo e das Carmelitas
Two churches, Igreja dos Carmelitas (1628) and Igreja do Carmo (1768), separated by a 1m house.

05 Kadoorie Mekor Haim Synagogue (1938)
Synagogue and museum of the Jewish community of Porto, the largest synagogue in the Iberian Peninsula.

06 Igreja dos Clérigos (1750)
Baroque church with 75.6m bell tower, designed by Nicolau Nasoni, who is buried in the church's crypt.

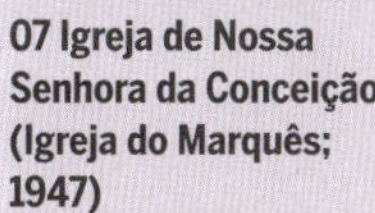

07 Igreja de Nossa Senhora da Conceição (Igreja do Marquês; 1947)

Asymmetrical church with both Romanesque and Gothic architecture, and grand views from the 50m tower.

08 Igreja de São Martinho de Cedofeita (1087)

Oldest church in Porto; rare example of a single-nave vaulted-ceiling temple.

09 Igreja da Lapa (1755, finished 1863)

Rococo and neoclassical, where the heart of King Pedro IV has been kept since 1835.

10 Capela Nossa Senhora da Silva (15th century)

Hidden Baroque chapel, the only one in Porto on the 1st floor, at Rua dos Caldeireiros 104.

11 Igreja de Santo Ildefonso (1739)

Covered by 11,000 tiles by artist Jorge Colaço in 1932, depicting biblical imagery and scenes from St Ildefonso's life.

12 Sé do Porto

Porto's cathedral dates to the 12th and 13th centuries, with a Roman-Gothic structure; some renovations were made in the Baroque period.

31 Porto from ABOVE

CLIMBING | VIEWS | WALKING

You've seen Porto at ground level, now it's time to tackle the city from a different perspective. Densely populated and hilly, Porto lends itself to a bird's-eye view, and the city offers a variety of ways to do this, from scaling one of the city's many bridges to more traditional viewpoints, and even a few free options.

SIRBOUMAN/SHUTTERSTOCK ©

How to

Locations The novelty experience closest to the centre is Porto 360 located in the Crystal Palace Gardens, followed by the Ponte da Arrábida climb (a stop on the 500 bus or short taxi ride), Serralves for the Treetop Walk (bus 203, Castelo do Queijo), then the lighthouse in Leça da Palmeira (20 minutes by taxi).

A moving panoramic view Take a ride in the Gaia Cable Car (gaiacablecar.com).

DIANA LOPES/SHUTTERSTOCK ©

SAIKO3P/SHUTTERSTOCK ©

Arrábida Bridge Climb (opened 2016: 262 steps, 65m, €16 to €17.50, 40 minutes) At one time the largest concrete arch in the world, Arrábida Bridge was completed in 1963 and is the last crossing on the Douro River before the ocean. Climbers ascend the arch towards sunset, taking in the views on either side; safety equipment consists of a harness and lifeline (portobridgeclimb.com).

Treetop Walk in Serralves (opened 2019: 260m of walkway, 1.5m to 15m in height, park ticket €12) The tree canopy provides a peaceful respite in the middle of urban Porto and gives visitors the opportunity to observe the biodiversity of the park. One-hour guided tours are provided in Portuguese, French and English, and there are family workshops on weekends (serralves.pt/en).

Porto 360 (opened 2021: 150 steps, €12.50, 40 minutes) Guided tours of the dome of the Super Bock Arena start with a history of the building from 1852 to the present day; then, visitors climb 150 steps to the top of the dome, where 360-degree views of the city await (superbockarena.pt/visitar/porto-360).

Monument(al) Views If your legs can manage it, we also recommend **Clérigos Tower** (75m, 240 steps, tower and museum €6, night pass €5); the much easier (and free) view from the **Portuguese Centre of Photography**; and the balcony of the **Mosteiro de Serra do Pilar** across the river (also free), part of Porto's UNESCO World Heritage Site, which includes Ribeira and the Luís I Bridge.

Left Super Bock Arena **Far left top** Gaia Cable Car **Far left bottom** Parque de Serralves Treetop Walk (p175)

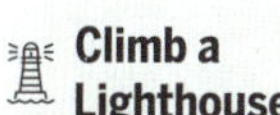

Climb a Lighthouse

A bit further afield, the most expansive view to be had is from the **Farol de Leça** (1926; amn.pt/DF/Paginas/FaroldeLeca.aspx), aka Boa Nova Lighthouse, in Leça da Palmeira, Matosinhos. At 46m, it is one of the tallest in Portugal, with a range of more than 50km of visibility on a clear day. Managed by the Maritime Police, the lighthouse can be visited for free (maximum six per group) from 2pm to 5pm Wednesdays, and 10am to 12.30pm on the first and third Sundays of the month.

32 Stroll Through History IN RIBEIRA

HISTORY | ART | PEOPLE

A UNESCO World Heritage site since 1996, Ribeira is one of Porto's oldest neighbourhoods, its narrow streets and ancient walls lining the bank of the Douro River. Today it's bustling with street performers, restaurants and bars, marine activity, and pedestrians soaking up the lively atmosphere.

Descent to the Douro

As parts of the embankment have steep inclines, this walk starts at the high point beside the top bridge deck and descends to the river by the stairs to save legs and lungs. If a cardio workout is desired, you may wish to do the itinerary in reverse.

Trip Notes

Getting around Ribeira is best explored on foot; some streets are very narrow and fill up easily.

Festivals & events Occasionally, major events shut down Ribeira, such as bike races, fun runs and the biggest annual celebration, Festas de São João, on the eve of 23 June.

Peak months Visitor numbers are especially high during July and August; crowds thin in spring and autumn, though the atmosphere remains lively.

0 200 m
0 0.1 miles
Jardim da Cordoaria
São Bento Train Station
05 Peruse **Casa do Infante**,
nuseum and alleged birthplace
f Henry the Navigator. Enter
he humming **Praça da Ribeira**,
ncient square and former trade
entre. A prime drinks stop.
01 Descend the ancient **Escadas do Codeçal**, part of the medieval wall with a view of the iconic Luís I Bridge. Pillars of the previous bridge, Antiga Ponte Pênsil, are still intact.
03 Outside the tunnel, browse **Ribeira Negra**, a 30m tile panel by Porto artist Júlio Resende, a Ribeira resident. Enter the **Barredo** quarter filled with colourful houses, narrow streets and *alminhas* (small sanctuaries).
R de São João
Av Vimara Peres
Jardim do Infante Dom Henrique
R Infante Dom Henrique
Pç da Ribeira
BARREDO
Duke of Ribeira
Av Gustavo Eiffel
R Alfândega
R de Fonte Taurina
Cais da Ribeira
Luis I Bridge
Barcos Náná
02 At street level, a memorial depicts **Tragédia da Ponte das Barcas**: the 1809 barge bridge which sank as thousands fled Napoleon; another honours river-rescue hero, the **Duke of Ribeira**, Deocleciano Monteiro (1902–1996).
Rio Douro
6 You've reached the
edieval wall **Muro**
s **Bacalhoeiros**,
rmer home of codfish
aders and birthplace
local dish *bacalhau*
Gomes de Sá; spot
e **Barcos Náná**
odel boats made
local character
rnando Teixeira.
04 Spot the **Torre do Barredo** (or Torre da Rua de Baixo) medieval civil architecture structure; note the markers recording the Douro River's major flooding events.
DENIS COMEAU/SHUTTERSTOCK ©, STOCKPHOTOSART/SHUTTERSTOCK ©

33 Urban Nature ESCAPES

PICNICS | VIEWS | GARDENS

Porto's municipal greens are a collection of historic gathering spots and modern landscape architecture, many with views to the water. Whether you're looking for a place to picnic, stretch out under the sun, people-watch or go for a walk, there's a park nearby to reconnect with urban nature.

SAIKO3P/SHUTTERSTOCK ©

How to

When to go Note that the walled and gated municipal parks have different closing times during the year, but typically close by sunset every day.

Events & markets Municipal parks often host events, plus weekend and seasonal markets for handicrafts, secondhand goods, food and speciality items (porto.pt/en/articles/category/culture).

Tip The only public toilets within any of the municipal parks in the historic centre are in the Jardins do Palácio de Cristal.

WIRESTOCK CREATORS/SHUTTERSTOCK ©

MICHAEL YK CHO/SHUTTERSTOCK ©

Historic Parks in the Centre

Jardim das Virtudes Formerly the Porto Gardens Company, its terraces give a 3D effect and sense of seclusion and privacy. It has great views to Alfândega do Porto (Customs House), the river and Vila Nova de Gaia.

Jardins do Palácio de Cristal Designed when the original Palácio de Cristal existed (19th century); peacocks wander freely. The park's municipal buildings include the Super Bock Arena Pavilhão Rosa Mota, Museu Romântico, an acoustic shell and the Almeida Garrett Municipal Library.

Jardim Marques de Oliveira Known locally as the garden of São Lázaro, this was Porto's first public garden in 1834. Built in a typical romantic garden style, it's great for people-watching.

Jardim de João Chagas Known locally as Cordoaria, from the days of rope-makers in residence from the 15th century. Another great location for people-watching; tram 22 runs through it.

Further Afield

Jardim Botânico Created in 1951, this was the former residence of the family of Portuguese writer Sophia de Mello Breyner Andresen. It's now part of the Museum of Natural History and University of Porto.

Parque da Cidade The largest urban park in Portugal (83 hectares), with restaurants, sports facilities, ponds, a museum and an event venue. There's a metro station nearby, making it fully accessible to wheelchair users using the network.

Left Jardim das Oliveiras **Far left top** Jardins do Palácio de Cristal **Far left bottom** Jardim Botânico

Jardim das Oliveiras

Opened in November 2013, Jardim das Oliveiras is both a green roof and park to replace Praça de Lisboa. With 4500 sq metres of grass and 50 olive trees, it is a perfect chill spot in this busy quarter, in view of Torre dos Clérigos, Lello Bookstore, the Rectory and Natural History Museum of the University of Porto. There is a bar and outdoor lounge as an alternative to the grass.

Port: A Fortified Nectar

AN OLD DRINK FOR A NEW WORLD

Four centuries of historical association with British merchants have given traditional port wine a reputation for being an older-generation tipple. But in modern times, port wine producers are diversifying their product lines, and targeting a wider audience and a younger demographic. Part of this includes integrating port wine into the food and drink scene.

Left Douro Valley vineyard
Centre Port tasting
Right Grapes on the vine

BARMALINI/SHUTTERSTOCK ©

Background

The term 'port' can only be used for fortified wine produced using grapes from the Douro Valley wine region, with quality control conducted by the Instituto dos Vinhos do Douro e Porto (IVDP). Port has been associated with the city of Porto for centuries, ever since the first port-shipping company was founded in 1638 by German ambassador Cristiano Kopke.

Port wine is created in the early stages of the winemaking process, when a neutral grape spirit is added to wine to halt fermentation, leading to a drink that has more residual sugar and higher alcohol content. After being fortified, some types of port wine are aged in bottles or barrels, traditionally in nearby Vila Nova de Gaia.

Grapes & Varieties

The grapes Most ports come from just six main grape varieties, but roughly 30 varieties can be used to make port.

Ruby port The fermented, fortified juice from red grapes undergoes some ageing and oxidation, leaving the fruity flavour and bright red hue of ruby port. Try it in poached pears, or pair it with chocolate truffles or goat's cheese after dinner.

Tawny port After being fermented and fortified, red wine is aged in wooden casks for at least three years, during which oxidation and evaporation provide the colour and distinct flavour profile of tawny port. This port can be consumed before dinner as an aperitif, with cheese and nuts during dinner, or as an accompaniment to dessert.

Vintage port Red wine from an exceptional harvest is fortified and aged in large barrels for a relatively short period of time, retaining its ruby hue and fruity flavours, before being

MATT MUNRO/LONELY PLANET ©

OLGA_GAVRILOVA/GETTY IMAGES ©

bottled. This type of port is aged in the bottle, not in the barrel. Walnuts or a strong cheese such as Stilton pair well with vintage port.

White port Made with white grapes, white port has been more in demand recently, as it is the main ingredient in *Porto Tónico*, a refreshing cocktail of white port mixed with tonic water and lemon – the perfect summer drink.

Port in Food

> Port has been associated with the city of Porto for centuries, ever since the first port-shipping company was founded in 1638.

Port wine is a common ingredient in *francesinha* sauce, and some well-known spots also use port wine as an ingredient in their glazes and syrups, as is the case for some versions of *rabanadas*, Portugal's decadent take on French toast. It's also a popular ingredient in desserts, from the very rich, sweet and traditional dish that is *pudim de Abade de Priscos* to fruit creations such as *pera bêbeda* (drunken pears) and *maçã assada com vinho do Porto* (roasted apples with port wine).

Speciality products such as onion-and-port-wine jam have become more mainstream, and port wine has traditionally appeared in Christmas recipes from *mexidos* and *formigos* (bread puddings) to *gemada com vinho do Porto* (eggnog) and *sonhos com calda de vinho do Porto* (pastries in syrup). Other local desserts that use port wine include *sopa seca* (literally 'dry soup'), a type of bread pudding that's enjoyed at Christmas and Carnaval, and during saints' festivals.

How to Enjoy Port Wine

Visit those who are passionate, including the small producers who believe their wines to be a reflection of their own time, of generations, of visions deeply rooted in the Douro. The genuine port wine devotee is the person who appreciates it, shares it, keeps it, drinks it with pleasure, who makes it immortal in special moments, turns it into cocktails, pairs it with food, desserts.

From glass to glass, from producer to producer, port wine becomes social and eternal.

Filipa Pereira and Moisés Campos, Wine Quay Bar *@winequaybar*

34 Port Wine LODGES

WINE | VITICULTURE | HOSPITALITY

Looking for port wine lodges in Porto? Called *caves* in Portuguese, they're located on the opposite riverbank, in Vila Nova de Gaia. Port society names such as Warre's, Taylor's, Sandeman, Ferreira and Graham's loom large over the warehouses and tasting rooms. The newest visitor centre is the World of Wine.

JAVARMAN/SHUTTERSTOCK ©

How to

Where to go Avoid crowds by visiting lodges further away from the river, as the closer ones are often included in packages with bridge cruise tickets.

Advance bookings If you are short on time or are part of a group, book a visit in advance.

Premium experiences If your port wine knowledge is advanced, skip the tour and upgrade your tastings for a premium experience.

BENNY MARTY/SHUTTERSTOCK ©

Far left top Graham's tasting room
Far left bottom Ferreira cellar

Tours & Tastings

Ever taken a port wine tour before? Be spontaneous and join the first tour that has free space. Guides will explain how port is made, why the Douro is a demarcated region and why the cellars are in Vila Nova de Gaia instead of Porto. You'll learn something about port, the city and Portugal's history at the same time. Tours typically involve 20 to 30 minutes in the cellars.

Many lodges have generations of winemaking in their families, and those stories can end up being the most fascinating part of the tour. Visits usually end in a tasting room and shop, where the guide will either commence an included port-wine tasting or give you a menu to make your wine selection. If you're buying port as a present, you'll probably want to extend your tasting – all in the name of research, of course.

If you are still undecided about which port lodge to visit, here are some for consideration: **Ferreira** offers the opportunity to learn about Dona Antónia Adelaide Ferreira, a powerful Portuguese businesswoman in a male-dominated industry; **Calém** ticket options include a fado show; **Graham's** is a tasting favourite and has one of the best views; **Real Companhia Velha** is the oldest wine company in Portugal (265 years); **Poças** is a notable smaller producer owned and operated by a Portuguese family

Taylor's Visitor Centre

Taylor's revamped their visitor centre in 2017 to a self-guided, exhibition-style space. Audio guides are provided in 12 languages with one to two hours of information, plus 30 minutes for the tasting of two ports. Information is formatted for a spectrum of wine knowledge, from novice to aficionado, with no reservations required.

35 A Day Trip to MATOSINHOS

SEAFOOD | ARCHITECTURE | WATERFRONT

Just north of the posh seaside suburb of Foz do Douro, Matosinhos is a genuine and gritty fishing port. It's worth considering a foot-based excursion here for the fresh fish and shellfish that comes straight off the boats – as well as for the interesting architecture and lovely beach.

Trip Notes

Getting around Take Porto's metro to and from Matosinhos; the walk itself can be done on foot.

When to go If you embark on this day trip in summer, combine it with a swim at Matosinhos Beach.

Top Tip Matosinhos is home to several surf-worthy spots, and surf lessons can also be arranged.

Something Fishy

Matosinhos was once home to 54 fish canneries. **Conservas Pinhais** is the only one of two still in operation. It opened in 1920 and underwent a renovation a century later, when it opened its Art Nouveau doors to guided tours of the facility. There's also a cafe and gift shop.

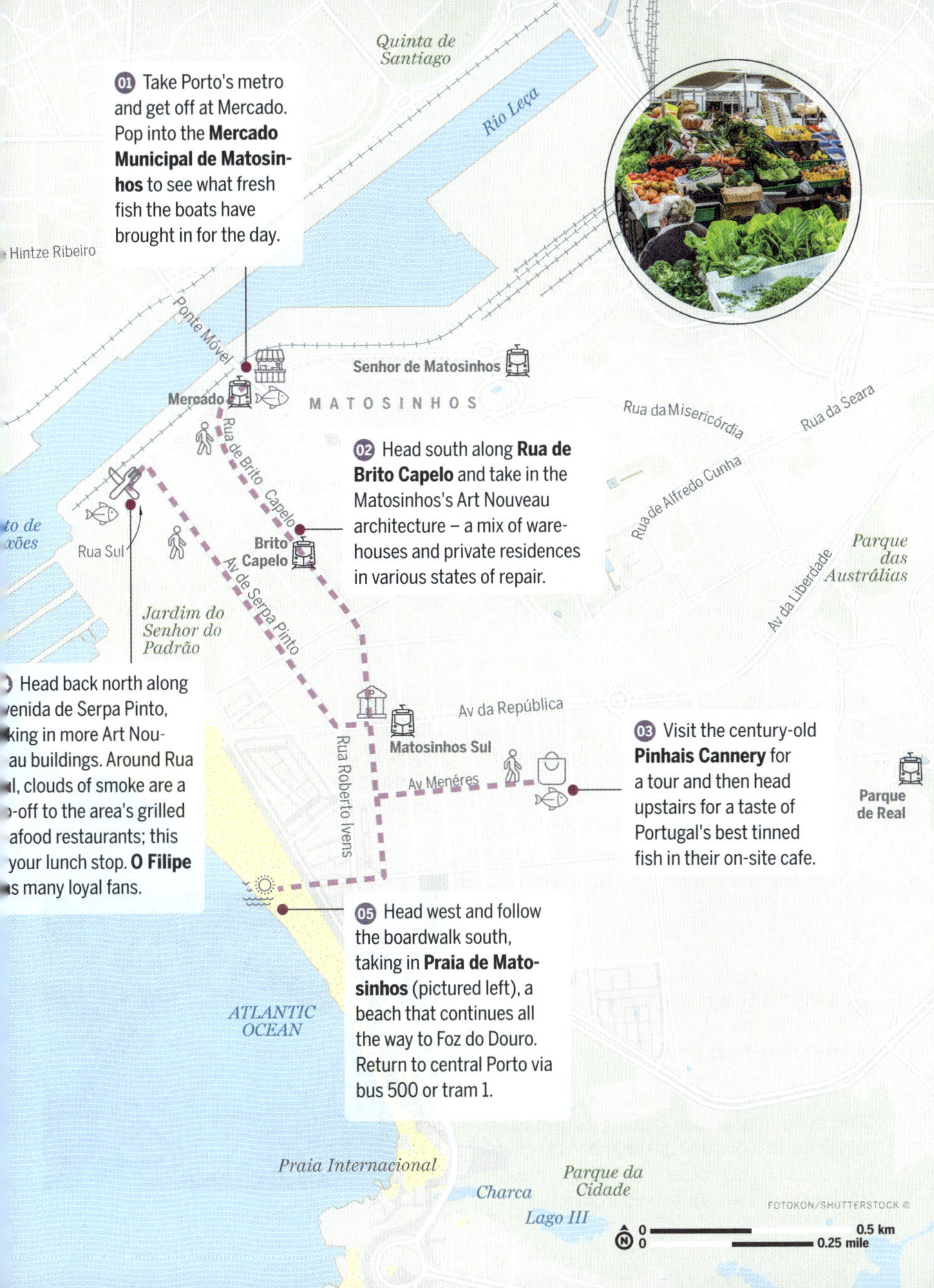

Quinta de Santiago
01 Take Porto's metro and get off at Mercado. Pop into the **Mercado Municipal de Matosinhos** to see what fresh fish the boats have brought in for the day.
Rio Leça
Hintze Ribeiro
Ponte Móvel
Senhor de Matosinhos
Mercado
MATOSINHOS
Rua da Misericórdia
Rua da Seara
Rua de Brito Capelo
02 Head south along **Rua de Brito Capelo** and take in the Matosinhos's Art Nouveau architecture – a mix of warehouses and private residences in various states of repair.
Rua de Alfredo Cunha
Rua Sul
Brito Capelo
Av de Serpa Pinto
Parque das Austrálias
Av da Liberdade
Jardim do Senhor do Padrão
Head back north along venida de Serpa Pinto, king in more Art Nouau buildings. Around Rua l, clouds of smoke are a -off to the area's grilled afood restaurants; this your lunch stop. **O Filipe** s many loyal fans.
Av da República
Matosinhos Sul
Rua Roberto Ivens
Av Menéres
03 Visit the century-old **Pinhais Cannery** for a tour and then head upstairs for a taste of Portugal's best tinned fish in their on-site cafe.
Parque de Real
05 Head west and follow the boardwalk south, taking in **Praia de Matosinhos** (pictured left), a beach that continues all the way to Foz do Douro. Return to central Porto via bus 500 or tram 1.
ATLANTIC OCEAN
Praia Internacional
Charca
Parque da Cidade
Lago III
FOTOKON/SHUTTERSTOCK ©
0 0.5 km
0 0.25 mile

Listings

BEST OF THE REST

Sundowner Spots

Genuíno €

Fun, Brazilian-run bar just north of the centre. There's an emphasis on Portuguese natural wines, but cocktails and vermouths are thrown into the mix, the latter a rarity in Portugal.

Capela Incomum €

Wine bar named 'Uncommon Chapel' and located in a 16th-century chapel (altar intact). Taste a wide range of Portuguese wines, with staff sharing the stories behind them.

Guindalense Futebol Clube €

Major points if you can find the entrance along a staircase (you'll pass by it if you take the Funicular dos Guindais). Simple, with great views; a classic Porto sports bar.

Musa das Virtudes €

Pull up a picnic table at the Porto branch of this Lisbon craft brewery for a glass from one of the 15 taps – and great views over the city.

Mirajazz €

Local wines and live jazz coupled with incredible views of the Douro River; located in Miragaia, it's a bit hard to find – climb the staircase across from the Alfândega car park.

Prova €

Diogo, the passionate owner of Prova, explains the finer nuances of Portuguese wine at this chic, stone-walled bar in Ribeira, where relaxed jazz plays.

Torto €€

This neon-infused den is doing its best to make Porto a cocktail destination via eccentric, delicious combinations made *na hora* (before your eyes) or served from a tap.

Terrace Lounge 360 – Porto Cruz €€

Fantastic rooftop lounge with grand views of Porto, located in the middle of Cais de Gaia. Porto Cruz (a port producer) hosts events in the building.

Dick's Bar – Yeatman Hotel €€€

Outstanding views of Porto and the Douro River coupled with the upscale service that's expected at the Yeatman. Exceptional drinks selection in a convivial atmosphere.

Epicurean Delights

Comer e Chorar por Mais €€

More than a century old, the aptly named 'Eat and Cry For More' is a well-known Porto delicatessen carrying regional products from around Portugal. Knowledgeable and friendly staff; tastings possible.

Garrafeira do Carmo €€

Specialty shop with varied inventory of all types of spirits, both domestic and imported; a wide variety of Portuguese wines with particular focus on port wine knowledge.

Comer e Chorar por Mais

Casa Natal €

Established in 1900, this traditional delicatessen sells typical Portuguese products such as confectionery, wine and olive oil. Located near Bolhão Market.

Arcádia €€

Traditional chocolatier of Porto since 1933, with several locations in Porto. Known for its bonbons, 'cat tongues' and Drageias de Licor Bonjour.

Leitaria da Quinta do Paço €

Originating as a dairy in Paços de Ferreira in 1920, this gem began making eclairs in the 1950s and grew from there. Six locations in the Porto area, mostly in shopping centres.

Mercearia das Flores €€

A fixture on Rua das Flores, this shop is part delicatessen, part cafe. It sells regional and organic Portuguese products.

Signature Sandwiches

Conga €

Located near Aliados, this hyper-casual spot specialises in *bifanas* – heavenly sandwiches stuffed with thin slices of pork that have been braised and drizzled with chili oil.

Casa Guedes €

Home of the *sandes de pernil* (oven-roasted pork shank sandwich). Don't skimp on the option that adds a slice of rich sheep's cheese. The original branch is at Praça dos Poveiros.

Gazela €

A short walk from São Bento Station, this is allegedly the origin of the *cachorrinho,* a crusty sandwich stuffed with sausages and cheese, griddled and brushed with spicy sauce.

Francesinha Café €€

This sultry place north of the city centre does a refined version of Porto's over-the-top take on the *croque monsieur.* Reservations recommended.

TRABANTOS/SHUTTERSTOCK ©

Praia dos Ingleses

Food Halls

Mercado Beira-Rio

No longer a traditional municipal market in Lower Gaia, this *mercado* resembles more of a food hall with kiosks operated as extensions of restaurants and food shops. Great for sampling various dishes.

Mercado do Bom Sucesso

Once a traditional market, the exterior remains the same, but vendors are now mostly food- and beverage-related. Also plays host to book fairs and occasional live-music events.

Time Out Market Porto

In 2024, *Time Out* took over a wing of Porto's São Bento Station, installing a dozen stalls as well as a tower that boasts a branch of the wonderful A Vida Portuguesa design shop.

Blissful Beaches

Praia dos Ingleses, Foz

Plenty of amenities around, accessible by public transport (bus 500 or 202) or on foot. Can be busy due to its convenient location. Bring layers in case of windy conditions.

Praia de Matosinhos

A 20-minute metro ride from Porto (get off at Matosinhos Sul). Find a beach bar and watch beach volleyball, surfing and the cruise ships at the Port of Leixões.

Praia da Madalena, Vila Nova de Gaia

One of Gaia's most popular beaches; on the other side of the Douro. Take bus 901 or 906 from Casa da Música and get off at the last stop.

Praia de Miramar, Vila Nova de Gaia

Home of the chapel on the beach, Capela do Senhor da Pedra (p180). A half-hour train ride from São Bento Station.

 Modern Architecture

Casa da Música

The 'House of Music' is an artistic, cultural and social venue designed by Dutch architect Rem Koolhaas for Porto 2001 European Capital of Culture. Guided visits daily, also in English, French and Spanish.

Porto de Leixões Cruise Terminal

Receiving cruise ships since 2011, the terminal was completed in 2015. It is also home to marina facilities, UPTEC/University of Porto, event rooms and restaurant. Guided tours on Sunday mornings (€5) from 9.30am to noon.

Serralves Villa

Located on the grounds managed by the Serralves Foundation in Boavista, the Villa is an example of 1930s art deco. Former residence of Count Carlos Alberto Cabral.

 Family Fun

Zoo Santo Inácio

A zoo built for the animals but also with families in mind, including picnic areas and restaurants. Visit all the different habitats in one entertaining day.

Parque Biológico, Vila Nova de Gaia

Cheaper than a visit to the zoo but just as educational. Find out more about the different animals and plants local to this region.

Clube de Minigolfe do Porto

Located at Jardim do Passeio Alegre, Foz (€2.50 for 18 holes). Have fun playing golf with your kids while watching the boats pass.

World of Discoveries

An interactive museum that presents Portugal's contribution to the exploration of the oceans and new routes to new worlds. Located across from the Customs Building.

Parque de Serralves

The Serralves Foundation organises the harvest festival and workshops for families. Go for a treetop walk (p183) or visit the farm animals.

Sea Life Porto

Walk through a tunnel under the main oceanic aquarium; find out more about other aquatic habitats including the Douro River and others around the world.

Casa da Música

Urban Art

Mira by Daniel Eime

This mural in Miragaia uses stencils to portray older local residents.

Half-Rabbit by Bordallo II

This magnificent sculpture is several storeys high and built from recycled rubbish; it's installed at the corner of a building in one of the back streets of Cais de Gaia.

Don Quixote by Mesk, Fedor and Mots

One of the first large-scale licensed murals in the city, it's located near Porto's main art street, Rua Miguel Bombarda (near Rua de Cedofeita).

Trindade mural by Hazul and Mr Dheo

The first big mural commissioned by the City of Porto from two of its most popular street artists at the time; it welcomes people to Trindade Metro Station.

Look at Porto by Vhils

This mural in Miragaia is on the 'Look at Porto' 5D cinema. The artist, Vhils, carved the white parts of the wall to produce it.

AN.FI.TRI.ÃO by Frederico Draw Alice Luísa Santos and Luísa Vieira de Sousa

Painted on the walls of a building behind the cathedral, this artwork welcomes those crossing the top of the Luís I Bridge from Vila Nova de Gaia.

Modern Religion by Mr Dheo

To counter the negativity usually associated with social housing, the city commissioned artists to paint murals in Francos and Carvalhido. This piece is in Francos.

Steak 'n Shake by Joana Vasconcelos

This mural, consisting of 8000 hand-painted tiles, was commissioned by the now-closed Steak 'n Shake restaurant.

DE VISU/SHUTTERSTOCK ©

Festas de São João

Local Events

Festas de São João

The *santos populares* (popular saints) all get their own day, and St John's is the eve of 23 June. Grill those sardines and get out your squeaky plastic hammer, because this is Porto's biggest party of the year. On 24 June there's a regatta on the Douro River, with a race between the port wine houses in their *rabelo* boats.

Festas de São Pedro

The end of June, usually, is when tiny Sâo Pedro de Afurada (Vila Nova de Gaia) celebrates St Peter with a parade, concerts and a street party.

Festas de Senhor de Matosinhos

Usually celebrated for several weeks in May, there's live music, street food, daily markets and an amusement park. This is an event for the whole family.

Festa do Outono, Serralves

The October harvest festival programme is for the whole family, with free access to the Serralves grounds.

Festival das Camellias

Typically held in early March. The city puts on a full programme of camellia-related events over several days; camellias were introduced to the city more than 200 years ago.

36 A Weekend in AVEIRO

ARCHITECTURE | OUTDOORS | FOOD

Art Nouveau architecture and a sprinkling of canals are bundled together in Aveiro's compact centre, just a short hop from its colourful, dune-backed coastline. And best of all, it's a 45-minute train ride from Porto, making Aveiro an easy weekend getaway.

DALIU/SHUTTERSTOCK ©

Trip Notes

Getting here Situated on Portugal's main train line, Aveiro has numerous easy connections with both Porto and Lisbon.

Getting around The municipality offers a free bike-rental service (with an ID deposit) from the BUGA kiosk, located near Mercado Manuel Firmino, Aveiro's main market.

When to go In March, temperatures start to rise, calling for festivities such as Aveiro's month-long Feira de Março, with bands, exhibitions and amusements.

Ovos Moles

Hailing from Aveiro's 17th-century convent, *ovos moles* combine sugar syrup and egg yolks, which were in abundance when the nuns would use egg whites for cleaning and housekeeping. The secret sweet recipe has since earned Protected Geographical Indication status, while their signature shell shape takes inspiration from the nearby ocean and lagoon.

04 Walk or bike to **Ecomuseu Marinha da Troncalhada**, an open-air museum where you can learn about the area's famous salt pans.

01 Aveiro is known for its Art Nouveau-style buildings. Kick off an architecture crawl at the **Museu Arte Nova** (closed Mondays).

02 Try *ovos moles*, Aveiro's signature sweet, at **Confeitaria Peixinho**, where the original recipe has been used since 1856.

05 Take a bus to Aveiro's coastal playground, which starts at **Praia de Costa Nova**, a 20-minute ride from the city. It's a beach known for its traditional *palheiros* (colourful striped cottages; pictured left).

03 Hop on a *moliceiro* from the **Moliceiros Pier** and enjoy these bright, colourful, high-prowed boats once used for gathering seaweed, now used for taking travellers on journeys along Aveiro's canals. Most trips last around 45 minutes.

37 Amazing Arouca GEOPARK

NATURE | ADVENTURE | HIKING

Rocky landscapes, river rapids and flora-veiled mountains welcome you to northern Portugal's UNESCO-listed Arouca Geopark. Over 40 geological attractions await scientific explorers, ranging from trace fossils to giant trilobites, while a network of 14 marked trails traverse the landscape.

PAULOMACHADO_9/SHUTTERSTOCK ©

How to

Getting here & around Driving to Arouca town takes one hour from Porto. Bus connections are approximately two hours with a change in São João da Madeira (€5.40; transdev.pt). To explore the park, utilise hiking routes, tours, taxis or self-drive.

When to go The walkways and bridge close on certain holidays. Spring and autumn are the most pleasant times for hiking. Snow can arrive on the coldest days.

Learn more The friendly Interactive Tourism Office provides maps for trails (aroucageopark.pt).

DE VISU/SHUTTERSTOCK ©

FILIPE PIMENTEL/SHUTTERSTOCK ©

Left Wildflowers, Arouca Geopark
Far left top Paiva walkway steps
Far left bottom Ponte 516 Arouca

Paiva walkways The serene soundtrack of river rapids and birdsong accompany you along the Passadiços do Paiva – Arouca's most treasured attraction. A near nine-kilometre linear trail of boardwalks, gravel tracks and wooden staircases follow the Paiva River, starting or ending at either Areinho (enter here if you wish to tackle the steepest stairs first) or Espiunca. River beaches, toilets and snacks can be found at either end, and also halfway at Praia Fluvial do Vau – while waterfalls and geosites, marked by information boards and QR codes, can be studied along the three-hour route. Taxis between trailheads and Arouca usually wait at both ends (€15 to €23), with the transfer time approximately 20 minutes (passadicosdopaiva.pt).

Ponte 516 Arouca Laying claim to being the world's longest pedestrian suspension bridge since opening in 2021, this 516-metre marvel of engineering stretches across the Paiva River. Crossing the metal grid-tray system 175m above the river is an exhilarating experience, and for those who dare, the views are reward enough (516arouca.pt).

River rafting adventures Once you've conquered the heights, and traversed the river walkways, add a little more adrenaline at water level by riding the rapids. Choose from rafting, canoeing and even river trekking by joining the local water-sports club for a day (clubedopaiva.com).

Booking & costs Tickets for Ponte 516 Arouca (€12 including the walkways) and Paiva Walkways (€2) are reserved online in advance.

The Park Beyond Paiva

Arouca town Marvel at the 17th-century Monastery and Sacred Art Museum, savour *castanhas doce* sweets or *Arouquesa* beef, and shop boutique stores for local handicrafts.

Hiking & biking Fourteen scenic trails cover various themes – such as geosites, waterfalls, cliffs or mines.

Panorâmica do Detrelo da Malhada Admire the spectacular verdant views over Serra da Freita from this raised platform.

Pedras Parideiras Interpretation Centre Learn more about the rare and fascinating process of granitisation from a 'mother' stone.

Canyoning & climbing Climb the rugged terrain in the Freita Mountain plateau or tackle one of nine canyoning routes through the park.

DOURO VALLEY
OUTDOORS | VITICULTURE | VIEWS

DOURO VALLEY

Trip Builder

Not just for wine lovers, the region offers a range of activities in every season, from summer vineyard events and guided museum visits to rejuvenating spring hikes. Relax in nature or feast on local gastronomy: the Valley's hospitality is legendary.

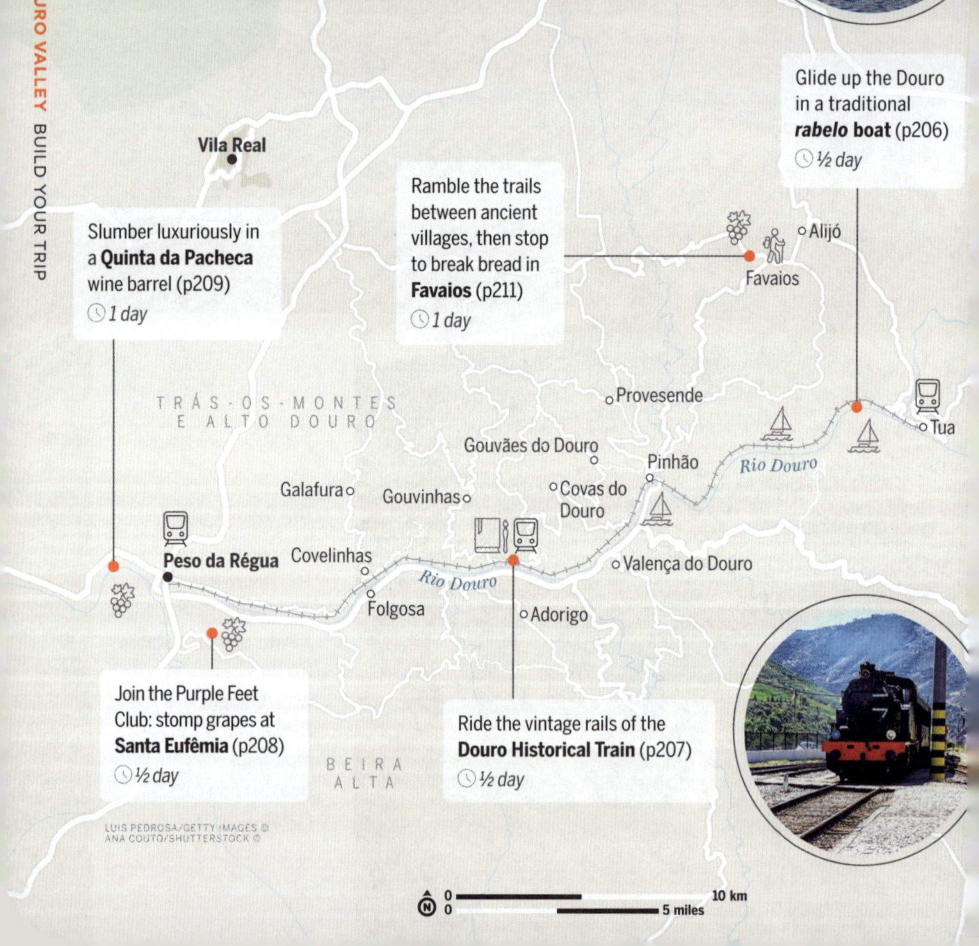

Glide up the Douro in a traditional ***rabelo* boat** (p206)
½ day

Ramble the trails between ancient villages, then stop to break bread in **Favaios** (p211)
1 day

Slumber luxuriously in a **Quinta da Pacheca** wine barrel (p209)
1 day

Join the Purple Feet Club: stomp grapes at **Santa Eufêmia** (p208)
½ day

Ride the vintage rails of the **Douro Historical Train** (p207)
½ day

Vila Real
Alijó
Favaios
TRÁS-OS-MONTES E ALTO DOURO
Provesende
Tua
Gouvães do Douro
Pinhão
Rio Douro
Galafura
Gouvinhas
Covas do Douro
Peso da Régua
Covelinhas
Valença do Douro
Folgosa
Adorigo
BEIRA ALTA

0 10 km
0 5 miles

Practicalities

ARRIVING

Porto Airport (OPO) is the closest, 100km from the Douro Valley.

Peso da Régua is a port city and hub for arrivals by train, boat, car and coach.

FIND YOUR WAY

Internet can be spotty in the Upper Douro; download a map locally in your GPS system or grab a detailed one in Peso da Régua.

MONEY

ATMs can be few and far between in the countryside. Carry enough cash for meals in small, family-run restaurants.

WHERE TO STAY

Location	Pros/Cons
Peso da Régua	Lots of lodgings; conveniently close to transport links.
Pinhão	Some options in Pinhão proper; many superb properties a short taxi ride away.
Lamego	Wider variety of accommodation, from wine hotels to guesthouses in town.
Vila Nova de Foz Côa	Charming rural lodges within half an hour's drive.

GETTING AROUND

Driving is the best way to visit the region.

Trains run on one line starting in Porto, following the Douro River on the north side, ending at Pocinho.

Intercity buses use a hub-and-spoke system, with Viseu the south hub and Vila Real the north hub.

EATING & DRINKING

Wine The choices are endless in wine country.

Traditional bread in Favaios is a bun with four corners.

Must-try convent sweets made with local almonds such as *tarte de amêndoa*.

Best bola de carne arguably *bola de carne de vinha d'alhos* of Lamego (the meat is marinated in wine and garlic).

JAN–MAR
Winter temps reach freezing overnight, March is moderate

APR–JUN
Best season to visit, especially April and May

JUL–SEP
Scorching days may curb activities; water and sunscreen essential

OCT–DEC
Chilly overnight; near freezing at altitude; daytime temps moderate

38 The Douro River from ALL ANGLES

TRAIN | BOAT | CAR

The majesty of the Douro Valley has inspired countless poets over the centuries. Most visitors take the train or road, but there are sections where neither get close to the water. With some of the most dramatic panoramas accessible only by boat from the river, here are some unique sightseeing options to consider.

HERACLES KRITIKOS/SHUTTERSTOCK ©

How to

Train *Linha do Douro* from Porto to Pocinho (€14.50, around 3½ hours; the only direct train leaves at 9am from São Bento Station in Porto). From Porto, sit on the right side as the train follows the river after Peso da Régua.

Car Avoid weekends in the summer if you wish to drive the EN222 between Peso da Régua and Pinhão as it can get congested.

***Rabelo* boat** Take the morning boat from Pinhão during the summer to avoid the worst heat in the afternoon.

JOSÉ RUI GALVAO/GETTY IMAGES ©

POIKE/GETTY IMAGES ©

See the Douro Your Way

The views of the Douro River are simply otherworldly between Pinhão and Pocinho – the most scenic section. So take a car, train or boat cruise that starts in Pinhão for unforgettable vistas.

Train Take the *Linha do Douro* from Porto, one of the most beautiful railway lines in Portugal. It was originally 200km when the full line was open (1872 to 1887), comprising 23 tunnels and 35 bridges. It is now 160km from Porto to Pocinho, the track mostly following the Douro River.

Douro Historical Train Time travel in a steam locomotive and five historical carriages between Peso da Régua and Tua. The line operates June to October (*cp.pt*).

Boat From Pinhão to Tua, choose from various types of watercraft, motorised or non-motorised. Departures can take place in the morning or afternoon, with trips from one to two hours or more. For a vintage experience take a *rabelo* boat, the traditional wooden cargo boat originally used to transport people and wine along the Douro River.

Car Hire a car and stop at the best viewpoints in the area. The only section where the road is next to the river is between Peso da Régua and Pinhão, but if you choose a weekday during the winter, you'll have it all to yourself. The 27km section of Estrada Nacional 222 between Peso da Régua and Pinhao was awarded the world's best road in 2015. Add your favourite road trip song and you'll want to drive this stretch again and again.

Left Pinhão **Far left top** *Rabelo* boat on the Douro River **Far left bottom** Barca d'Alva

Landscapes From a Kayak

Seeing the Douro Valley from a kayak is a profound experience. Paddling past the terraced hills in the morning silence is very special. Between Barca d'Alva and Pocinho where there is no road or train, the silence is only broken by the birds singing and the fish jumping.

■ **Jack Atkinson**, Douro Kayak *dourokayak.com*

39 The Path of Wine ESTATES

TRADITION | WINE | ESTATES

The wine producers of the Douro Valley number in the thousands, from tiny operations closed to the public to large, established estates opened year-round to visits. How to choose? We have selected five notable wine estates, listing them geographically from west to east.

PEDRO QUARTIN GRACA/SHUTTERSTOCK ©

Trip Notes

Getting around The first three *quintas* (Pacheca, Vallado and Santa Eufémia) are an easy taxi ride apart, while the last two (Bomfim and das Carvalhas) are across the Pinhão Bridge from each other, which can be crossed on foot.

When to go Visit year-round, but during harvest time the grape-stomping is a one-day event, which should not be combined with other visits.

Top tip Eat plenty and hydrate – port wine is 22% alcohol content!

The Purple Feet Club

Making wine is hard work! The workers sing to make stomping more enjoyable, following the same rhythm and pace to crush the slippery grapes. We recommend staying next to the vines at Santa Eufémia's visitor lodge in Parada do Bispo, which will make it easier to participate.

Vila Real

TRÁS-OS-MONTES E ALTO DOURO

02 Quinta do Vallado is one of the oldest in the valley with both a traditional house and a modern schist building, with pool, gardens and spa. Impressive winery and coveted location.

05 Quinta do Bomfim's prized wines demonstrate the local obsession with the winemaking process. Located in the Upper Douro, the estate is both traditional and contemporary, with quality tours and tastings.

Provesende

Pinhão

Galafura

Gouvinhas

Covas do Douro

Peso da Régua

Covelinhas

Rio Douro

Valença do Douro

Folgosa

Adorigo

03 Quinta de Santa Eufémia is a relatively small, seventh-generation producer next to a charming, newly refurbished chapel. Observe their entire production line through glass; if timed right, it's possible to arrange grape-stomping.

04 Quinta das Carvalhas is a classic estate with unique views of the Douro River. It's possible to spend the whole day there with activities – they even have a birdwatching programme.

BEIRA ALTA

01 Take a relaxed tour of 18th-century **Quinta da Pacheca** followed by a wine tasting, and stay in one of the *quinta's* 10 giant barrels (pictured left) – more luxurious than you'd think!

0 5 km
0 2.5 miles

40 Wine Villages RECLAIMED

OUTDOORS | VILLAGES | HIKING

In 2001, when the Douro wine region was given UNESCO World Heritage status, a project with the aim of recovering several wine villages was born. Six were chosen for rehabilitation: two of them on the north side of the Douro, four on the south, all with the Douro countryside as their backdrop.

How to

Getting here It is easier to get around by car; there is no bus service to these small villages.

When to go It can get insanely hot for hiking in the summer. Spring and autumn are the best months for temperature and flora.

For tranquil walks Avoid the peak of the harvest season: vineyards are busy and with all the machinery, it can get quite noisy.

Far left top Favaios **Far left bottom** Ucanha bridge

Provesende This rural wine village was once the seat of a municipality. It boasts several manor houses, most notably Morgadio da Calçada, which is partly open to the public. Other points of interest include the pillory, the 17th-century fountain, the 18th-century Church of St Marinha and the Portuguese-Roman cemetery at Quinta da Relva.

Trevões Traditional shoe-making is still alive and well here. The historic centre has ancient houses and two museums, one dedicated to the village and countryside, the other to religious art.

Barcos Sloping above the Távora River, Barcos is known for its views and the 12th-century church with interesting porticos, one of the best examples of late-Romanic architecture.

Salzedas and **Ucanha** are villages less than 3km apart, with a maximum of 100m elevation change, making for an easy amble.

Salzedas has an impressive monastery of the Cistercian Order whose construction first began in 1168 and expanded in the 17th and 18th centuries. Try the Salzedas biscuit *(biscoito de Salzedas)*, the traditional recipe of the Cistercian monks who also made elderberry liqueur.

Ucanha is one of the oldest settlements in the region. The village is unique in Portugal for its toll tower and medieval fortified bridge over the Varosa River. Stop by the Church of São João Evangelista and the ruins of the Old Abbey.

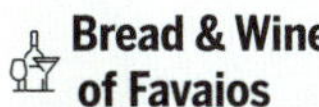

Bread & Wine of Favaios

The village of **Favaios** may be small, but it's become a favourite stop for visitors to the Douro Valley.

Visit the **Favaios Wine Cooperative** (Adega Cooperativa de Favaios) to sample Moscatel wine and learn about its production.

The informative **Bread and Wine Museum** (Núcleo Museológico Favaios, Pão e Vinho) is another place to dive into the history and traditions of the local area. You'll also learn more about Moscatel and the process of baking the local speciality, four-cornered bread. The museum gives tastings of the bread and Moscatel produced by the local cooperative.

41 Rock Your IMAGINATION

ARCHAEOLOGY | NATURE | ROCK ART

The Côa Valley Archaeological Park, in the Upper Douro where the Côa River branches south, is a 200-sq-km open-air gallery of prehistoric rock art, the largest concentration in the world today. The park was created in 1996 to preserve and manage its exhibition to the public. The expansive Côa Museum was added in 2010.

ARCHITECTS: CAMILO REBELO AND TIAGO PIMENTEL TAKASHI IMAGES/SHUTTERSTOCK ©

How to

Getting here The closest coach stop is Vila Nova de Foz Cõa, about 3km from the museum. The *Linha do Douro* stops at Pocinho train station, 7km from Vila Nova de Foz Côa. The *Linha da Beira Alta* stops at Celorico da Beira train station, 60km from Vila Nova de Foz Côa.

Prearrange visits Visiting the archaeological sites is only possible by prearrangement with the museum.

ANDERS BLOMQVIST/GETTY IMAGES ©

ROBERT SZYMANSKI/SHUTTERSTOCK ©

Left Rock art inscriptions **Far left top** Côa Museum **Far left bottom** Visiting the Côa Valley Archaeological Park

The large and modern **Côa Museum** is situated on a rocky outcrop at the intersection of two UNESCO World Heritage sites where the rivers Côa and Douro meet. Digital media exhibitions illustrate the art of the prehistoric engravers to complement the major works, the archaeological sites. The museum also has a restaurant.

There are three main sites to visit: **Canada do Inferno**, **Penascosa** and **Ribeira de Piscos**. In addition to the rock art sites open to the public, there are other archaeological sites nearby worth visiting: Roman and medieval ruins, castles and remnants of other settlements.

Kayak visits to Canada do Inferno or Fariseu combine a relaxing leisure activity with rock art, flora and fauna. Fariseu boasts the largest outdoor engraving of 3.5m, which can only be viewed by kayak.

Canada do Inferno and Ribeira de Piscos are visited only during the morning, when the panels are illuminated by the sun. For the same reason, the engraved panels at Penascosa are visited only in the afternoon. Night visits, which use light and shadow to make the engravings stand out, are only available at Penascosa. Note that visits to Penascosa depart from the village of Castelo Melhor, at the park's reception centre.

Bouncing in a 4WD at the edge of steep ravines feels like going on a safari, with eagles and vultures circling overhead. The protected park is home to various species of flora and fauna, mostly undisturbed by human contact. There's an aura of mystique owing to its wild, rugged nature.

Right This Way

The only access to the archaeological sites at Parque Côa is by prior arrangement with the museum, which limits the number of visitors for conservation and practical reasons. Visits to the three main sites can be undertaken on foot along marked pedestrian trails, through organised kayak trips, or excursions in all-terrain vehicles, followed by a walk to the engravings.

The museum guides have specialised training, and can identify and explain the etchings in the schist rock. These are mainly of the early animals that roamed the Côa Valley, namely aurochsen (a species of wild cattle), horses, goats and deer species.

Listings

BEST OF THE REST

Top Castles in the Douro

Lamego

Medieval castle documented since the 10th century. This is the highest point in Lamego with the best views of the Coura, Balsemão and Varosa Rivers. Today what remains is the keep (tower) and walls.

Freixo de Espada à Cinta

One of the oldest castles in the area, documented since the 13th century. Today there are some remains of the old fortress, mainly the seven-sided Torre do Galo.

Numão

Medieval castle dating back to the days of the Christian Reconquest and impressively illuminated at night. It's believed that the castle once had 15 towers and was often visited by kings.

Events & Festivals

Festa da Amendoeira em Flor de Vila Nova Foz Côa

The Almond Blossom Route (*Rota das Amendoeiras em Flor*) puts on a show from late February to early March when the Douro Valley blooms. It is a wonder to behold when driving from Vila Nova de Foz Côa (Portugal's capital of almond trees) to Barca d'Alva. This coincides with the annual two-week festival programme hosted by Vila Nova Foz Côa, culminating in a parade on the last day.

Romaria da Nossa Senhora dos Remédios (Lamego)

This large-scale event is held from late August to early September in Lamego, in honour of Our Lady of Remedies. There are fireworks, shows and the Procession of the Triumph by pilgrims on 8 September.

Vindouro – the Pombaline Festival (São João da Pesqueira)

Three days in late August to early September celebrate all things wine: from competitions, auctions and tastings to an 18th-century street market. Other activities include concerts, a traditional Pombaline market, a parade and dinner prepared by a well-known Portuguese chef. On the last day, 1 September, there's an auction of historic wines.

The Douro's Viewpoints

São Leonardo de Galafura

Thirty minutes by car from Peso da Régua and 640m high, the view was an inspiration for the Portuguese poet Miguel Torga (real name Adolfo Correia da Rocha).

Casal de Loivos

Between Pinhão and Alijó in the village of the same name, where the vineyards, farms and villages hug the river and form a landscape that will take your breath away.

Douro Valley seen from São Leonardo de Galafura

Fraga do Puio

Located in Picote, the viewpoint is within the Parque Natural do Douro Internacional along the border between Portugal and Spain. The balcony was rebuilt in 2017 in glass and wood.

São Salvador do Mundo

Located at a height of 493m near São João da Pesqueira, the vista overlooks the Douro Valley and its smaller rivers, the dam and the Cachão da Valeira.

Rota do Douro

Located between Beira and Coleja, across from Quinta das Vargellas and Vargellas railway station, with magnificent views over the villages and vineyards.

Dining With Flair

DOC, Folgosa €€€

The crème de la crème of dining experiences in the Douro is by chef Rui Paula, who has twice received Michelin stars since 2017. DOC (Degustar Ousar Comunicar; Taste Dare Communicate) opened in 2007 and has a coveted view of the river. The menu is a reflection of the valley's abundance and seasonality.

Cozinha da Clara, Pinhão €€€

Executive chef Pedro Cardoso started Cozinha da Clara in 2017. Part of the wine estate Quinta de la Rosa near Pinhão, it prides itself on using produce from its own garden and sourcing ingredients as locally as possible, and has a menu which leans contemporary.

Wine House Restaurant, Lamego €€€

Chef Carlos Pires heads the restaurant located in Quinta da Pacheca, in a rural setting opposite Peso da Régua on the left bank. The restaurant menu is Mediterranean and traditional Portuguese, with world influences such as French and Japanese styles weaving their way in.

TRABANTOS/SHUTTERSTOCK ©

Museu de Lamego

Museum Picks

Museu do Douro, Peso da Régua

Completed in 2008, this regional museum in a renovated 18th-century building represents the wine region's collective identity and cultural attributes. It houses a permanent collection and an exhibition space, plus a restaurant, a store, an information centre, a reading room, a wine bar and an esplanade in a garden with a view of the Douro River.

Côa Museum, Vila Nova de Foz Côa

Opened in 2010, this museum has four floors of permanent and temporary exhibitions dedicated to the prehistoric rock art of the Côa Valley, and the environment of hunter-gatherer societies in the Paleolithic era.

Museu de Lamego

Once an episcopal palace, this museum is in the historic centre of Lamego and was inaugurated in 1917. It contains an eclectic collection of artefacts from photography to transport, and textiles to paintings.

42 Detour to MINHO

NATURE | WINE | HISTORY

Charming villages, the country's only national park, legendary wines, deep historical roots and seemingly never-ending shades of green: consider this corner of northwestern Portugal for a multi-day visit that touches on the best the country has to offer.

LEV LEVIN/SHUTTERSTOCK ©

How To

Getting here The train is one of the best options for visiting hubs like Viana do Castelo, Braga and Guimarães.

Getting around Driving maximises your exploration of the Minho region in terms of time, ease and coverage.

When to go With cooler temperatures, spring is ideal for hiking and other nature-related activities, while the warm summers are best spent at the beach.

NANDI ESTEVEZ/SHUTTERSTOCK ©

Charming Towns & Cities

Viana do Castelo sits on the verdant coastline of Costa Verde, drawing beachgoers, windsurfers and hikers alike. The interaction between the river and the sea is a pivotal part of its identity and industry: it's still a land of fishers, sailors, *sargaceiros* (sargasso harvesters) and shipyard workers.

Braga teems with churches and ruins spanning over 2000 years of history while simultaneously enjoying a cosmopolitan vibe and booming cultural scene. The city is also regarded as the country's religious epicentre, hosting Portugal's oldest cathedral, **Sé**.

Guimarães, the nation's birthplace, is home to a pristinely preserved historic centre, a flurry of monuments, delicious food and excellent museums.

TANIAARAUJO/SHUTTERSTOCK ©

The Rooster of Barcelos

Legend has it that a pilgrim was wrongly condemned to death. His desperate father called on the rooster the judge was eating and told him to sing if his son was innocent, and he was saved. Today, manufacturing these black-dotted roosters is a tradition in Barcelos.

Top left Braga church **Top right** Pitões das Júnias (p218) **Left** Parque Nacional da Peneda-Gerês (p218)

Natural Areas

One of Minho's biggest draws is the **Parque Nacional da Peneda-Gerês**. It's Portugal's only national park, and spans more than 700 sq km of emerald-green lagoons, camouflaged waterfalls and secluded stone villages.

The park's northern section is home to tiny villages and forests. Adventure sports, hiking and swimming in the lagoons can be enjoyed in the park's centre. The park can also be used as a jumping-off point for explorations of the ancient granite houses of **Pitões das Júnias**, or the terraced hillside village of **Sistelo**.

Wine Country

Monção and Melgaço share a particular Atlantic micro-climate. The weather has shaped this corner of the *vinho verde* region, giving birth to one of the nation's most famous white grape varieties: Alvarinho. It's here that Alvarinho wines reach their peak of perfection, and visits to the wine estates of **Palácio da Brejoeira** and **Quinta de Soalheiro** are simply unmissable.

The Celtic Influence

The *cultura castreja* (hillfort culture) was prevalent in northern Portugal and Galicia between the Bronze Age and the 1st century CE. The *castro* is a fortified settlement, protected by granite walls and moats, and filled with round houses.

Thousands of *castros* have been identified in the Minho and Trás-os-Montes regions. Due to constant invasions, the northern Iberian populations were forced to live in isolation and in a permanent defensive state. When the Romans conquered the Iberian Peninsula, they changed the organisation of the *castros*, creating defined neighbourhoods and public infrastructure.

The area around Ponte de Lima is also home to a *vinho verde* sub-region. **Quinta do Ameal**, an 18th-century farm, is in close proximity to the gushing Rio Lima, and the vineyards are surrounded by dense forest. **Aphros Wine**, pioneers in biodynamic winemaking, are creating a new generation of wines made with local varietals.

Prehistory

Minho is home to several Iron Age settlements, known as *citânias* or *castros*.

Perhaps the most accessible is the one that towers over Viana do Castelo. **Citânia de Santa Luzia** displays a cautious defensive structure, lined by three walls with towers and moats. Inside, you can observe the foundations of over three dozen houses, most of which display typical circular architectural features and the odd bread oven. The incredible views are no coincidence: its strategic location allowed the population to control all entries into the Lima estuary and surrounding land.

A 30-minute drive from Guimarães is **Citânia de Briteiros**, one of the most important landmarks of Iberian protohistory. Partially hidden by woodland, the hillfort overlooks the Rio Ave. Within the lichen- and moss-laden defensive walls and cobblestone streets, you can see remnants of Iron Age life, all the way back in the 10th century BCE.

Left Citânia de Briteiros
Below Citânia de Santa Luzia

TRÁS-OS-MONTES
OUTDOORS | HISTORY | LOCAL HERITAGE

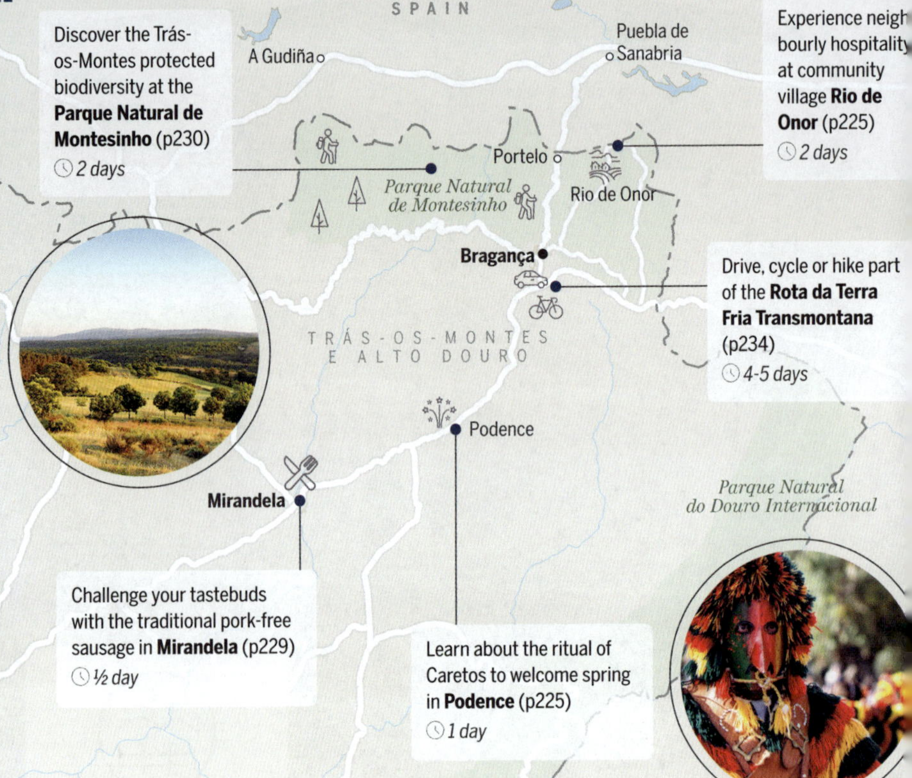

TRÁS-OS-MONTES

Trip Builder

The isolated location and infamous weather of the northeast – the *Nordeste Transmontano* – have created an intriguing cultural identity. Embrace the *transmontano* lifestyle by exploring protected natural parks and enjoying ancient pagan celebrations.

Practicalities

ARRIVING

Porto Airport (OPO) is the closest, a three-hour drive via the A4 motorway.

Express buses from Porto and Lisbon serve most of the main towns.

CONNECT

Good wi-fi coverage. Double-check your plan fees: near the border, your phone might pick up a Spanish carrier's signal.

MONEY

Carry cash for small purchases at local shops. Chain stores and other businesses accept most debit and credit cards.

WHERE TO STAY

Location	Pros/Cons
Bragança	The district's capital city; mix of boutique hotels and well-known international chains.
Rio de Onor	Picturesque, self-catered rural homes for short-term rent; community lifestyle in the village.
Vinhais	Camping at Parque Biológico de Vinhais; free facilities; bring your campervan or your tent, or stay at bungalows.

GETTING AROUND

Driving is the best way to get to know Trás-os-Montes, via a mix of high-speed roads and scenic, undulating secondary toll-free byways cutting through the mountainous landscape.

Long-distance buses depart with some regularity from Lisbon and Porto to the main cities in the northeast. A network of almost 80 municipal bus routes connects all cities, towns and villages in Trás-os-Montes.

TOP: NATALIA MYLOVA/SHUTTERSTOCK © BOTTOM: FILIPE B. VARELA/SHUTTERSTOCK ©

EATING & DRINKING

Feijoada à transmontana A hearty bean-based stew cooked with cabbage and smoked meat.

Castanha da Terra Fria Locally produced chestnuts, DOP (Protected Designation of Origin).

Wine Fruity whites and robust reds with Ancient Roman roots await in the Valpaços sub-region.

Must-try local dish
Alheira at O Grês (p236)

Best for Posta Mirandesa
Gabriela (p236)

JAN–MAR
Expect snow in alpine areas and rituals welcoming spring

APR–JUN
Mild temps with chilly mornings and evenings, ideal for outdoors

JUL–SEP
Scorching days call for swims at river beaches

OCT–DEC
Winter starts to settle in; great for spending time indoors

43 Community VILLAGES

NATURE | COMMUNITY | TRADITION

Out of almost two dozen traditional villages scattered all over the *Nordeste Transmontano*, at these four, community life is more prominent and local traditions ignore the passage of time. Isolation brought on by long, hard winters and geographical constraints may have crystallised the way of living of these villagers, but they are still very much connected to the outside world.

RUI T GUEDES/GETTY IMAGES ©

How to

Getting here If you're driving, take the A1 (from Lisbon) or the A4 (from Porto). Express buses go as far as the neighbouring cities of Macedo de Cavaleiros and Bragança.

When to go Snowscapes and traditional Carnaval celebrations in February/March make winter the best season to visit.

Experience village life Briefly become part of the community by staying at a self-catered, independent house *(alojamento local)* in any of the villages.

DIEGO MATTEO MUZZINI/SHUTTERSTOCK ©

Rio de Onor With fewer than 100 permanent residents, this tiny village of typical houses, farmland, herds and a shared oven is two towns in one. Split by the border, its Spanish side is called Rihonor de Castilla, but locals dismiss political boundaries and divide it into the top part (Rihonor) and the bottom part (Rio de Onor).

Chacim Located at the foot of the Serra de Bornes, this village was chosen by royal decree in the 18th century to breed silkworms, and produce and weave silk. Chacim became one of the main players in Portugal's industrialisation efforts. These days, however, only ruins and memories remain of the old silk factory, Real Filatório de Chacim.

Podence At the end of 2019, this village near Macedo de Cavaleiros jumped to international attention as their traditional way of celebrating Carnaval became officially part of UNESCO's Intangible Culture list. The *Entrudo Chocalheiro* is a pagan celebration in which men wearing colourful hooded suits and *caretos* (tin or leather masks) bid the long winter farewell and welcome the rejuvenating spring.

Montesinho At about 1030m above sea level, this village in the heart of the Parque Natural de Montesinho is one of the highest in Portugal. The houses, some restored and transformed into tourist lodgings, maintain their typical thick granite walls, slate roofs and wooden balconies – ideal for enduring the heavy snowfalls of winter.

Far left top Rio de Onor **Far left bottom** Montesinho

Explore Beyond the Villages

Visit 'France' without leaving Portugal About 10km separates the villages of Montesinho and França. Weather permitting, hike the marked trail between the villages, among the protected landscapes of the natural park.

Local river beach The Azibo river beach (Praia Fluvial da Ribeira) near Podence is a top recommendation among locals. The Blue Flag beach is also equipped for beachgoers with reduced mobility.

Build your own careto mask The farm-turned-hotel Quinta do Pomar (quintadopomarmaior.com/en) houses a workshop where visitors can see how a *careto* mask is made and give it a shot themselves.

By Teresa Vivas
Teresa has worked in agricultural production and founded Portugal's first gastronomic marketing agency. @tecasmaria; @mesa_cultura_gastronomica; @mais_madeira_a_mesa

The Winter Table

IN ALTO TÂMEGA AND BARROSO, WINTER IS THE HAPPIEST TIME OF THE YEAR

The fireplace, known as the smokehouse, warms the days with delicious food and camaraderie among village neighbours and friends. Miguel Torga, one of the greatest Portuguese writers, called this region the 'Marvellous Kingdom', and upon visiting, you'll truly feel like you're in a different realm.

Left *Alheira*
Centre *Cozido* **Right** *Salpicão*

Unlike most traditional cuisines, which peak in summer and autumn, in Trás-os-Montes, Alto Tâmega and Barroso, it's during harsh winters that the full richness of the local produce is revealed.

For many Portuguese, Trás-os-Montes was an almost unreachable territory until shortly after the year 2000. Because of its forced isolation, the pig is still 'worshipped' in this corner of Portugal. The pigs are fed from the gardens with cereals and chestnuts, and are treated with the utmost care throughout the year in order to enhance the quality of the meat. At the first signs of cold weather, the festive days begin. Spices, seasonings and techniques honed over generations are used to make the best sausages and cured meats in the village. Each household has its own unique seasoning, and the excitement of the winter sets in.

In every home, the frost is welcomed and the white mantle of snow awaited; here, the smokehouses take centre stage: sausages, blood sausages, hams, ears, tails and muzzles are cured and become sources of joy. The *Tabernas do Alto Tâmega* are special tables set up in the homes of the farmers, allowing visitors to eat and experience unique moments: these homes become small restaurants that offer the simplicity of life in the deepest rural environment.

Each feast begins with grilled *alheiras* – queen of the smoked sausage –made with wheat bread, olive oil, lard, garlic and various parts of the pig. Other meat like poultry or rabbit can also be included. *Salpicão* – another staple at the table – is made from leaner meats and sliced very thinly. But the king of the table is the ham, usually made with the extreme care and personal taste of the host, who can spend up to two years curing it.

NATALIA MYLOVA/SHUTTERSTOCK ©

EDUARDO MIRANDA RAMOS/SHUTTERSTOCK ©

The room where the hams are cured is almost always cool, often doubling as a wine-ageing spot. Visitors are welcome to taste these delicacies, but it's recommended to assure the host that their ham is the best you've ever tasted. The bread is dark rye with an unmistakable aroma, and the *folares* – dough embedded with sausages and smoked meats – is hard to resist.

The cold and rain bring out wild mushrooms in the woods, which are turned into irreplaceable *petiscos* (snacks). The chestnut orchards provide shade and food, with the chestnuts fried, boiled or roasted by the fire. From the garden, cabbages – softened by the frost – become sweet and tender, just as the people of Trás-os-Montes prefer them. The potatoes, produced by local growers, rest in dark, cool stores and are reputed to be the best in the country.

> In every home, the frost is welcomed and the white mantle of snow awaited; here, the smokehouses take centre stage.

The dishes from Alto Tâmega are hearty, comforting and substantial: many could be mentioned, but *cozido Barrosão* stands out. The only meat present is smoked pork (feet, muzzle, ear and fatty cuts like bacon), and it's combined with cabbage, potatoes, beans, plus various sausages, including blood sausage. Other notable dishes include smoked sausage rice, Barrosã or Maronesa steak on the grill, roast kid and various codfish dishes, always seasoned with the finest olive oil.

This is just a glimpse of the Alto Tâmega and Barroso winter table...only here can you eat like this!

The Perfect Ending

All meals here conclude only when the French toast is served. Made in the classic way but finished with local honey that is rich with the deep, strong flavours of heather, chestnut and broom, the dessert is served warm and scented with cinnamon.

44 Cuisine & Craft TRADITIONS

FOOD | ARTS | CULTURE

More than just trying local dishes or selecting must-buy traditional souvenirs, embrace the cuisine and craft experiences of this region. Artisanship highlights the incredible qualities of the people of *Nordeste Transmontano*: their resilience, resourcefulness and resolve in keeping traditions alive.

HORACIO VILLALOBOS/GETTY IMAGES ©

How to

Getting here Driving is your best bet. All villages, towns and cities are connected by an intricate network of motorways (autoestradas) and secondary roads (marked as N, IP or IC).

When to go Local celebrations, which involve food and traditional cultural events, are at their peak during winter.

Alternative foods Traditional cuisine is meat- and game-heavy, but it's possible to find vegetarian alternatives to some staple dishes.

SAIKO3P/SHUTTERSTOCK ©

VICVA/SHUTTERSTOCK ©

Left Smoked sausages, Feira do Fumeiro **Far left top** Pauliteiros de Miranda **Far left bottom** Wine barrels

Well-Seasoned Local Culture

A deceiving sausage When, in the 15th century, Iberian Jews were forced to convert to Christianity or else face persecution, most became New Christians on paper but continued to practise their religion in secret. The absence, however, of a staple dish like pork (which is forbidden in Jewish diets) in someone's household would raise suspicion. So, the Jewish community in Mirandela invented *alheira,* in which poultry and bread replace pork in this garlicky, paprika-flavoured sausage. Another version of the tale, though, states the sausage was born out of scarcity of the usual main ingredient.

Unattractive but delicious Made with bean pods and a type of local sausage, *butelo com cascas* is a traditional stew in which the smoked flavours make up for the lack of love at first sight.

From a village to the world Of the almost 600 people who live in Palaçoulo, a town in Miranda do Douro near the Spanish border, most live off the cutlery- and barrel-making industries. Instead of giving in to their geographical isolation, villagers made the best of their traditional knowledge, turning artisanal knives and wine barrels into a booming, international business.

Northeastern music instruments Traditionally built and played by shepherds, the Mirandese bagpipes are one of the rarest and oldest of their kind in Europe. They're part of the soundtrack of many traditional cultural events and have made their way into the contemporary Portuguese music scene.

Local Feasts & Festivals

Feira do Fumeiro
Vinhais, self-proclaimed capital of smoked meats, hosts an event solely dedicated to local sausages every February (www.cm-vinhais.pt).

Festival do Butelo e das Casulas The peculiar bean pod and sausage stew is the main attraction of this event in Bragança, but festival-goers will also be able to indulge in other local delicacies.

Pauliteiros de Miranda
True to their Celtic roots, Pauliteiros replaced swords with sticks in a traditional dance, accompanied by local bagpipes. In addition to an ongoing application for UNESCO's Intangible Cultural Heritage list, the ensemble represented Northern Portugal at Expo 2020 Dubai (pauliteiros.com).

45 Outdoor DELIGHTS

STARS | SNOWSCAPES | BIODIVERSITY

Prepare to ditch the stress of urban life at the country's largest protected area, Parque Natural de Montesinho. Meander through the picture-worthy landscapes of the Portuguese northeast, hike or cycle the marked paths, observe the resident wildlife, gaze at starry skies or enjoy the first snowfalls.

ANDERS BLOMQVIST/GETTY IMAGES ©

How to

Getting here Bragança is the city closest to the Parque Natural de Montesinho, a 30-minute drive away. Driving is the best way to get around.

When to go Spring and autumn are the sweet-spot seasons for outdoor enthusiasts and wildlife Connoisseurs. Snowy winters are best for time indoors.

Protected by UNESCO Since 2015 the park has been part of the Meseta Ibérica Transboundary Biosphere Reserve, the largest in Europe.

MATT MUNRO/LONELY PLANET ©

Animal-spotting

As one of the most biodiverse natural parks in Portugal, Montesinho is the home of almost 70% of the country's total species, some of them endangered. During your wildlife encounters, planned or otherwise, respect their habitat, give them space, make sure your clothes blend in with the colours around you as much as possible, and admire them from a safe distance.

September to October is mating season for the deer. It's a haunting, one-of-a-kind experience as the sounds of their mating calls echo through the park. To increase your odds of witnessing this event, visit the park early in the morning.

Iberian wolves, one of the aforementioned threatened species, roam freely through the hills of Montesinho, hunting deer and wild

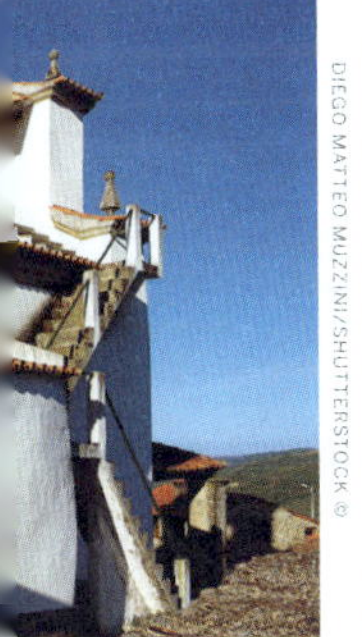
DIEGO MATTEO MUZZINI/SHUTTERSTOCK ©

Overnight in Aldeia de Montesinho

For a fully immersive experience, stay at one of Montesinho village's typical houses, which have been converted into self-catered short-term rentals. In winter, the snow-covered village is even more appealing. During Christmas, witness the ancient pagan rituals celebrating the winter solstice.

Above left Parque Natural de Montesinho **Left** Montesinho church **Above right** Village farmhouse

boar, bred to maintain this delicate ecosystem. They are one of the most important populations of Iberian wolves in the country.

With more than 100 resident species of nesting birds, the Parque Natural de Montesinho is the chosen permanent address for a few couples of golden eagles. Other birds of prey such as black storks and hen harriers join them in their choice of home.

When treading the hills or the trails, pay close attention to every body of water that you come across. The park houses half of all the reptile and amphibian species living in Portugal.

The resident mammals, such as wildcats, otters, bats and European water voles, take over abandoned mines and mills scattered around the park.

Explore Beyond the Park

Ancient Roman path In Moimenta, past the medieval Ponte das Vinhas, notice the relatively well-preserved path, which is thought to have been built by the Ancient Romans.

Núcleo Interpretativo da Lorga de Dine In Dine, a village about 10km from the Parque Natural de Montesinho, visit this local museum showcasing Neolithic archeological artefacts that were found in the neighbouring cave.

Mel do Parque de Montesinho Honey exclusively produced in Montesinho has held the DOP (Denominação de Origem Protegida; literally 'Protected Designation of Origin') label since 1994 and has been certified organic since 2005 (meldoparque.webnode.pt).

Left Roman bridge, Moimenta **Below** Hikers, Parque Natural de Montesinho

Hiking Trails

The Parque Natural de Montesinho has two official hiking trails, both circular and ideal for hikers who are okay with a route that is a little challenging. Because the park is a preserved area, travellers must stay on the marked trail at all times.

The **PR3 BGC – Porto Furado** trail begins and ends at the typical village of Montesinho, stretching for 7.8km through valleys, rivers, reservoirs and hilly landscapes. It's the ideal route for nature enthusiasts, more immersive and with fewer stops. The highest peak, Alto do Falgueirão, rises almost 2000m above sea level. At the final stop, before returning to Aldeia de Montesinho, spot the ruins of the Iron Age settlement Castro Curisco.

Starting in Moimenta, the **PR7 VNH – Calçada** trail is the same length as the Porto Furado, but has two more stops, most at human-made landmarks. The mix of attractions on this route favours diverse travelling groups. It balances natural beauties, like the view from Miradouro de Moimenta and the largest forest of oak trees in Europe, with architectural heritage must-sees, like Ponte das Vinhas (a medieval bridge over River Tuela) and Igreja Matriz de Moimenta (the 14th-century main church in the town where the trail ends).

46 Encounter the ROTA DA TERRA FRIA

ROAD TRIP | HIKING | CYCLING

The Rota da Terra Fria Transmontana is 455km long, split into 11 pre-designed, independent itineraries of varying lengths. So prepare for unforgettable first impressions of the Portuguese northeast while hiking, cycling or driving this condensed, inland itinerary.

RIBEIROANTONIO/SHUTTERSTOCK ©

Trip Notes

Getting here You can start the itinerary in Bragança, a gateway city to the Rota. Get there by bus or car from Lisbon or Porto.

When to go Hikers and cyclists should plan for a spring trip. Summers are scorching, so it's best to travel by car then.

Take the detours The official route map marks detours to unmissable points of interest, from quasi-secret viewpoints to monuments and landmarks.

Route Within the Route

If you're keen on exploring a less crowded part of the Camino de Santiago, the route overlaps with the Rota da Terra Fria in Sobreiró de Baixo (a 45-minute drive from Bragança). The Portuguese section of the Camino begins there.

04 Take a foodie detour in **Vinhais** (pictured left), a town known for its smoked meats and hearty soups. In October, locally produced chestnuts are the main stars of food event Rural Castanea.
SPAIN
01 Before heading off, or at the end, carve out time to pay a visit to the 900-year-old medieval castle, protected by a heart-shaped wall, in **Bragança**, and the city's historic centre.
Portelo
Vilar Seco de Lomba
Parque Natural de Montesinho
Vinhais
Bragança
02 Approximately 52km down road N217, stop in the small village of **Izeda** to taste (and buy) Trás-os-Montes' unique olive oil produced locally.
05 Near the end of Rota da Terra Fria, in **Vilar Seco de Lomba**, vineyards take over the landscape. Peel your eyes for *bodegas* – wine cellars semi-buried in schist rocks.
Salsas
Podence
TRÁS-OS-MONTES E ALTO DOURO
Izeda
Rio Sabor
Rio Tua
Parque Natural do Douro Internacional
03 In the village of **Salsas**, stop by the old train station to admire the colourful tile panel honouring the local *caretos*.
Rio Douro
0 20 km
0 10 miles
N

Listings

BEST OF THE REST

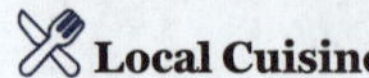

Local Cuisine

Gabriela €€

Family-owned for almost a century, this typical restaurant at the heart of Sendim was the first to serve what would become one of the region's most famous steaks: *posta Mirandesa*.

Moagem João do Padre €€

This restaurant on Rua do Porto, Podence's main street, serves hearty traditional food in generous portions. Make sure you save room for its well-loved chestnut pudding.

Flor de Sal €€

At this riverside restaurant in Mirandela, traditional recipes are prepared and served using contemporary techniques. The roast lamb is one of its most famous dishes.

Taberna O Batoque €

Not all Transmontana cuisine is meat-based. This restaurant in Bragança designed a traditional menu around vegetarian and vegan-friendly mushrooms, another popular ingredient in the Portuguese northeast.

O Grês €€

Skip asking for the menu at this traditional restaurant in Mirandela, for there's only one dish that makes patrons flock here: the home-style *alheira*.

Cultural Immersion

Museu Ibérico da Máscara e do Traje

At this museum in Bragança's historic centre explore the history of the Iberian winter celebrations through permanent exhibitions of traditional masks, props and costumes. Closed on Mondays.

Festival Intercéltico de Sendim

Lovers of folk music head to Sendim every year in early August to attend this 20-year-old international festival dedicated to the Celtic-based genre.

Carnaval de Podence

One of Portugal's most traditional and unique Carnaval celebrations takes place in Podence. The three-day festivities welcoming spring culminate on Shrove Tuesday with the Caretos' parade and the burning of an effigy.

Centro de Interpretação da Cultura Sefardita do Norderdeste Transmontano

This small, local museum in Bragança documents the several Jewish communities that have lived in the Portuguese northeast over the centuries. Closed on Mondays.

Centro Interpretativo do Real Filatório de Chacim

At the village of Chacim, this interpretative centre helps to make sense of the historical legacy of the former silk factory now in ruins. Open all year round. Book a guided tour at the *posto de turismo* in Macedo de Cavaleiros.

Museu Ibérico da Máscara e do Traje

Walk the wine or Roman routes

Valpaços' city council designed two self-guided walking routes around the region's most important cultural legacies: wineries carved in rocks and ancient Roman roads (valpacos.pt/pages/555).

 Local Crafts & Food

Cutelaria Martins

Established in 1954, this family-owned factory in Palaçoulo is well known for its customisable artisanal pocket knives. Other types of knives are also available to purchase online or directly at the local store.

Quinta do Pomar

At Podence's main street, in addition to selling local food products, this local *mercearia* sells merchandise related to Caretos: handmade tin and leather masks, cow bells, and the tradition-based board game.

MARRON – Oficina da Castanha

Taste and buy chestnut products at this local business in central Bragança with a museum, a grocery store and a 30-seat cafeteria where this fruit rules the menu.

Gaita de Foles Mirandesa

The Mirandese bagpipes are part of most of the region's popular music soundtracks. Crafted by hand, the process to build one of these instruments is methodically slow. Célio Pires (Constantim, Miranda do Douro) is one of the most reputable artisans.

 Prehistoric Settlements

Castro de Sacóias

A 15-minute drive from Bragança, the remains of an Iron Age settlement near Capela Nossa Senhora da Assunção almost go unnoticed.

MAURICIO ABREU/ALAMY STOCK PHOTO ©

Trás-os-Montes musicians with traditional bagpipes and drums

After several restructures, it was presumably occupied last by Roman settlers.

Miradouro e Povoado Fortificado da Ciradelha

Not much is left of this prehistoric settlement, a 10-minute drive from Vinhais. But the view and the historical information on-site make up for the absence of identifiable remains.

Castro de Ciragata

Also known as Cidadelhe de Parada. The ruins of a defensive wall are visible atop a hill, a short drive from the village of Parada (Bragança district). Archaeological findings confirmed its Iron Age origin.

Mamoa de Donai

Practically destroyed megalithic monument 300m to the west of Donai, a village about 10km from Bragança. Resort to locals to pinpoint the exact location of this unmapped landmark.

Abrigos Rupestres do Regato das Bouças

Rock shelters near the Bouças stream in Mirandela, probably used between the Neolithic and Chalcolithic periods, according to the drawings found on-site.

Practicalities

Right Tuk-tuk (p243), Lisbon

EASY STEPS FROM THE AIRPORT TO THE CITY CENTRE

Lisbon is the primary point of entry for most travellers visiting Portugal. The airport is about 6km from the city centre. All flights, domestic and international, arrive at Terminal 1. Terminal 2 is used for departing flights by low-cost carriers. There are some cafes and shops in the arrivals hall, but there is greater variety in the central plaza, on your way to baggage claim.

AT THE AIRPORT

SIM CARDS
Cards for unlocked phones can be purchased at the Vodafone Portugal shop at baggage claim (7am to 6pm). However, if you want to compare prices, wait until you've reached the city centre and look for an MEO or NOS shop, the other two Portuguese mobile operators.

CURRENCY EXCHANGE
Unicâmbio offices are located at baggage claim (5am to midnight) and in the arrivals hall (5am to 1am). However, exchange fees are higher at the airport. If you don't need cash right away, get better prices at other Unicâmbio stores or banks in the city centre.

BENNY MARTY/SHUTTERSTOCK ©

WI-FI Free wi-fi is available at both terminals, but is usually slow and unreliable. Select _VINCI Airports WiFi and follow the prompts.

ATMS Teller machines are operated by SIBS (known as *Multibanco*) or Euronet (typically charges hefty fees). Both are available throughout the airport.

CHARGING STATIONS Dedicated stations are not available. The few wall sockets you'll find are typically overused or defective. Bring your own powerbank.

ENTRY FORMALITIES

Valid ID European Union or Schengen area citizens must travel with a valid identification document (Citizen Card). A valid passport and visa are required for other citizens.

Visas can be waived, depending on the visitor's country of origin.

GETTING TO THE CITY CENTRE

Metro The Red Line connects the airport to Alameda (Green Line), Saldanha (Yellow Line) and, the final stop, São Sebastião (Blue Line). The station is a few steps from the arrivals hall, to your right. Buy tickets from automatic vending machines or ticket offices at the station.

Bus Several city bus lines stop at the airport arrivals terminal. Note that the maximum baggage size allowed in these buses is 50x40x20cm. Find details at carris.pt.

Taxi Pick-up areas are outside the arrivals zone. Not all taxis take credit or debit cards. All fares are metered.

Ride-share Pick-up area for ride-shares is in the 2nd floor parking garage; upon entering the arrivals hall, turn left.

Viva Viagem Purchase a travel card (€0.50) at vending machines or ticket booths at the metro station.

Top up with money not by number of trips. You can use the card across all public transit in Lisbon (metro, bus, tram, lifts, train and ferry) without worrying about how much each trip costs.

Minimum top-up is €3. Maximum is €40.

OTHER POINTS OF ENTRY

Other airports you can fly into are Porto (closer for exploring the north) and Faro (best for travellers spending time in the south: the Algarve and Alentejo). The other international airports are located on the islands: Funchal (Madeira) and Ponta Delgada (São Miguel, Azores).

International cruises arrive at Lisbon Cruise Terminal near Alfama, at the heart of Lisbon's historic centre. Sometimes cruise ships dock in Alcântara or Rocha do Conde de Óbidos instead (approximately 10km from the city centre; call an Uber or take trams 15E or 18E to Cais do Sodré).

International buses operated by Rede Expressos arrive from several Spanish destinations at Lisbon (Sete Rios; connects to the Blue Line and suburban trains), Faro and Porto (Campo 24 de Agosto).

International trains connect Vigo (Spain) and Porto (Campanhã). There's also talk of restarting the direct overnight train that used to link Lisbon and Madrid.

TRANSPORT TIPS TO HELP YOU GET AROUND

To cover more land and visit remote inland areas, driving is your best option. You're not dependant on restrictive public transit schedules (some areas are only served by bus twice a day, in the morning and in the evening) and you get to stop along the way to simply admire the views or follow your urge to take a detour.

CAR HIRE

Typically, car-rental companies charge rates per 24 hours, not a calendar day. Automatic transmission cars are in short supply and typically more expensive; most cars in Portugal are manual.

AUTOMOBILE ASSOCIATIONS

ACP – Automóvel Clube de Portugal (acp.pt) – is a good resource for road maps, queries about insurance and driving rules, tolls and how much they cost, travel and accommodation tips, and all you need to know about camping in Portugal.

CAR RENTAL PER DAY

Train tickets If you don't mind planning your trip far ahead, CP – Comboios de Portugal (the national railway company) – cuts long-distance train tickets by up to 56% for passengers buying an Alfa Pendular or Intercidades ticket at least five days before departure, within Portugal. Tickets are available to purchase on the website (cp.pt) or via the mobile app. You must create an account and add your credit card or PayPal details.

BICYCLE The number of cycle paths is increasing in Portugal, from scenic bike routes by the coast to a robust network of bike lanes in main cities. Bring your own or rent one when you arrive.

ROAD CONDITIONS Paid-toll motorways (*autoestradas*) and high-traffic secondary roads (IPs and ICs) are generally in good condition. Smaller, toll-free roads (N or EN) are usually narrow, curvy in mountainous areas, and poorly lit at night.

DRIVING ESSENTIALS

Drive on the right.

At toll booths pay with a debit card or change. If you're renting a car, ask for the Via Verde tag to use the fast lane.

Speed limit is 50km/h in urban areas; 90km/h when driving on secondary roads; 120km/h on motorways.

.05 Blood alcohol limit is 0.5 g/l.

18 Legal driving age is 18 years.

BUS & TRAIN Along the coast, most towns and cities are well-served by a reliable and comfortable network of trains and long-distance buses. Popular destinations inland are easy to reach by bus, but rail has lacked investment in recent years, meaning that some stations are permanently closed. At the time of writing, Portugal was yet to have a fast-train connection to the rest of Europe.

TUK-TUKS A popular way of getting around in Lisbon, tuk-tuks are not to be confused with public transit. Typically, they solicit clients near attractions. Prices can be high for short distances; not all drivers are skilled.

PLANE TAP and several budget carriers operate regular domestic flights from Lisbon to Porto (55min) and Faro (45min). Tickets are not always cheap, so weigh the pros and cons of going through an airport against a comfortable and hassle-free train trip.

KNOW YOUR CARBON FOOTPRINT A car trip from Lisbon to Porto would emit 70kg of carbon dioxide per passenger. The same one-way trip by bus would emit 34kg of carbon dioxide per person. A train ride would emit 19kg of carbon dioxide.

There are a number of carbon calculators online. We use Resurgence at resurgence.org/resources/carbon-calculator.html.

ROAD DISTANCE CHART (KMS)

	Lisbon	Porto	Braga	Bragança	Évora	Sintra	Setúbal	Óbidos	Olhão
Porto	314								
Braga	364	55							
Bragança	486	207	217						
Évora	133	365	415	462					
Sintra	29	330	382	504	153				
Setúbal	48	349	399	521	98	69			
Óbidos	85	241	290	418	195	97	122		
Olhão	285	559	608	730	234	306	252	350	
Faro	277	551	600	722	226	298	244	342	10

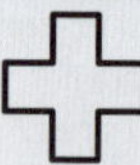

DANGERS, ANNOYANCES & SAFETY

Portugal is a relatively safe country. Crime rates are low. Observe the same precautions regarding your belongings as you would back home. Pickpockets and scammers usually gather around popular attractions and try to pass off as tourists in a crowd.

SCAMS Popular scams in the larger cities include raising funds on the street for local charities that don't exist, in exchange for a fixed-fee photo. And selling 'drugs' openly during daytime, particularly in touristy, pedestrian-only streets. The only thing these fake dealers are selling is pressed bay leaves and flour.

CANNABIS Portugal decriminalised the use and possession of all drugs, regarding addiction as a disease not a crime. Being caught with a up to 25 grams of cannabis for personal use is not a crime.

THEFT Mind your belongings when exploring a busy place on foot and don't leave any valuables showing inside your rented car. Pickpocketing, stealing purses and vehicle break-ins are the most common occurrences. They're mostly non-violent crimes of opportunity perpetrated by several people working as a network, targeting wallets, mobile phones and other electronic devices.

Pharmacies sell prescribed and over-the-counter medication; Parapharmacies only sell over-the-counter drugs in smaller dosages. If you're in need of paracetamol or plasters, you can safely get them at either.

STUDIO F22 RICARDO ROCHA/SHUTTERSTOCK ©

LEISA TYLER/GETTY IMAGES ©

Solo travel With such a low crime rate, Portugal is the third safest country in the world and one of solo travellers' favourite destinations. That said, observe the same safety precautions you would back home.

INSURANCE

Insurance is not compulsory to travel to Portugal but it's good to have. Consider one that covers flight cancellation and medical care. Alternatively, or additionally, EU travellers can apply for the European Health Insurance Card.

FOREST FIRES

Hot, dry, windy summers and unsustainable agricultural practices are the perfect spark for 'fire season'. Travellers should check the latest IPMA reports on wildfire risk at ipma.pt/en/risco incendio/rcm.pt.

QUICK TIPS TO HELP YOU MANAGE YOUR MONEY

CREDIT CARDS Visa and Mastercard are accepted at larger chain hotels, supermarkets, cafes and restaurants, and for car rentals. Small businesses prefer cash or payments with debit cards for bills over €5 (they pay a fee for each transaction, with no extra cost to you). Businesses that don't accept cards usually display a sign stating so. Diners Club and American Express cards are not as widely accepted.

ATMS

ATMs are practically on every corner in larger cities. Smaller towns and villages might only have them at local bank branches.

CURRENCY EXCHANGE

Change currency at banks or at licensed money changers (Unicâmbio) at the airport, tourist spots or shopping centres.

CURRENCY

Euro (€)

HOW MUCH FOR A...

espresso coffee **€0.75**

glass of wine **€3–5**

3-course dinner for 2 **€20–30**

TIPPING is optional and not expected.

Restaurants Most restaurants don't include service charges in your bill. If you want, reward good service with a 5% tip.

Taxis Round up the fare and tell the driver to keep the change.

Guides If you want to reward spectacular service, consider giving your guide an extra €5 to €10.

VAT REFUND Non-EU residents can claim a VAT (IVA in Portugal) refund for certain purchases at places boasting the Tax Free Shopping sign. Apply at the airport.

TOURIST TAX

Travellers staying in Lisbon and Porto must pay €2 per person per night, up to €14 per person (Lisbon) or maximum seven nights (Porto). The tax is often included in your accommodation bill.

PAYING THE BILL

Most cafes have table service. Others have a pre-payment system. At busier establishments, staff hand you a card with your registered orders to pay at the counter when you leave.

DISCOUNTS & SAVINGS

Most sights, activities and public transport charge a reduced fee to seniors, children under 12 and families.

City cards The Lisboa Card includes unlimited free public transport, free entry to selected museums and attractions, and deals on tours. Starts at €26 (24-hour card). Similar benefits are included in the Porto.CARD. Prices start at €13. Both cards can be purchased online and must be exchanged for a physical card at the airports' tourist information booths.

POSITIVE-IMPACT TRAVEL

Tips to leave a lighter footprint, support locals and have a positive impact on communities.

ON THE ROAD

Calculate your carbon footprint There are a number of online calculators. Try resurgence.org/resources/carbon-calculator.html.

Disposable, single-use plastic As of July 2021, Portugal has banned single-use plastic. Follow the lead and use reusable bags, cups and water bottles where possible.

Tap water is safe to drink in most of Portugal. When in doubt, ask a local.

When hiking or cycling stay on the marked trails and don't disturb the local wildlife.

Forest areas are susceptible to wildfires, especially in summer. Be careful with cigarette butts if you're a smoker; all it takes is a small spark to start a fire.

Public transport Strike up conversations with locals (football is always a good topic) by using public transport. Support local taxis wherever possible.

BIRDSNLANDSCAPE/SHUTTERSTOCK ©

GIVE BACK

Volunteer with a Portuguese-based social enterprise Check ongoing projects and locations at impactrip.com.

Sponsor a donkey Support local NGO Aepga in protecting the Mirandese donkey (pictured), an endangered species. See aepga.pt.

Support contemporary artisans Up-and-coming Portuguese artisans are adding modern twists to traditional techniques. Check portugalmanual.com for a list of artisans to support.

Experience a rural tourism stay The surge of farms-turned-hotels prevented rural areas from becoming deserted. Consider spending some time at one of those accommodations or booking a farm tour via portugalfarmexperience.com.

Donate two hours of your time Give back by collecting food that would go to waste and giving it to those who need it most. Find out how at re-food.org.

DOS & DON'TS

Do queue if you see everyone else doing it. If in doubt who's the last in line, ask.

Don't wear your bathing suit or shorts outside of the beach area.

Don't discuss politics, religion or sport without context or reassurance from the other side that they're ready to talk about it.

LEAVE A SMALL FOOTPRINT

Get to know the the bin colours Recycling bins are widely available in large cities. Green is for glass, yellow is for plastic and packages, and blue is for paper.

Practise mindful van life Park your van at official campsites. As much as it sounds romantic to wake up to a different view every day, illegal parking disturbs local human and wild life.

Plant a tree Visit plantarumaarvore.org to make a donation to plant one or more trees that are suitable for Portugal's environment and eco-balance.

IMREN TUTUNCU/SHUTTERSTOCK ©

SUPPORT LOCAL

In cities and large towns choose small businesses over large chains, both national and international.

Eat locally Buy fresh ingredients at local markets or eat at small, family-owned restaurants with traditional food. Eat a great-value soup and sandwich combo at a cafe instead of a fast-food joint.

Buy souvenirs from local artisans Ask the local *posto de turismo* for a list of shops and ateliers.

CLIMATE CHANGE & TRAVEL

It's impossible to ignore the impact we have when travelling, and the importance of making changes where we can. Lonely Planet urges all travellers to engage with their travel carbon footprint. There are many carbon calculators online that allow travellers to estimate the carbon emissions generated by their journey; try resurgence.org/resources/carbon-calculator.html. Many airlines and booking sites offer travellers the option of offsetting the impact of greenhouse gas emissions by contributing to climate-friendly initiatives around the world.

RESOURCES

zero.ong
natural.pt
quercus.pt
impactrip.com
re-food.org

UNIQUE AND LOCAL WAYS TO STAY

***Accommodation in Portugal has room for all tastes and budgets, from self-catered rural homes to city-centre hostels to restored castles turned into luxury hotels. And although hitting the road in a campervan seems to be the new fad, it's nothing new for families used to summers at* parques de campismo.**

HOW MUCH FOR A NIGHT IN

a country home
€90

a hostel dorm
€30

a guesthouse
€60

RADIOKAFKA/SHUTTERSTOCK ©

ALOJAMENTO LOCAL

Although often used to classify short-term rentals available on platforms like Airbnb, Alojamento Local (AL) is an umbrella term used to designate guesthouses. At this type of accommodation, breakfast is usually not provided or comes at an extra cost, private bathrooms might be optional, there is no 24/7 front-desk service and in-room amenities are limited. They're often located in the city centre or near main tourist attractions.

Rates start at approximately €60 per night in high season.

YOUTH HOSTELS & HOSTELS

While youth hostels mostly cater to students and large groups who don't mind sharing a dorm, hostels come in many shapes and sizes. You'll find a blend of dorm, private (shared or not) and family rooms. Rates vary depending on the season, but expect to pay around €30 for a dorm bed.

POUSADAS DE PORTUGAL These are a network of old monasteries, convents, forts, castles and palaces transformed into luxury hotels by the Pestana Group. Despite the modern facilities, each hotel respects the history and architectural traits of the former monuments.

Prices vary according to location, but rates start at around €150 per night.

STOCKPHOTOSART/SHUTTERSTOCK ©

MIGUEL ALMEIDA/SHUTTERSTOCK ©

LOCAL CONNECTIONS

From entire villages that have been transformed into rural tourist resorts to working family farms and wine estates, opportunities for meeting and staying with locals are myriad. Although all differing in size and facilities, the emotional or family relationship with the place is central to the character of these lodgings. Expect close contact with the community, through locally sourced products at your breakfast table, and traditional arts and crafts.

RURAL TOURISM

Whether you want to unwind, reconnect with nature or fill up your days with outdoor adventures, make your trip memorable by staying at a privately owned country house. They come in all shapes and sizes: country hotels (HR – *Hotéis Rurais*), old manors and palaces (TH – *Turismo de Habitação*), small country houses (CC – *Casas de Campo*) and farmhouses and wine estates (AG – *Agro-turismo*).

Book in advance around peak season, long weekends and national holidays. A large breakfast of local products is usually included. Other meals may be provided upon request.

Prices vary depending on the size of the room, but start at about €70 per night in peak season.

BOOKING Book in advance during peak season (mid-June to mid-September, Easter and Christmas) and long weekends. Check local and national holidays that fall on a Thursday or a Tuesday – locals often take a vacation *ponte* (bridge) day on Friday or Monday.

Aldeias de Portugal (aldeiasdeportugal.pt) A website listing most of the village tourist resorts in the country.

Solares de Portugal (solaresdeportugal.pt) Book a stay at a restored family manor, estate or country house.

Pousadas de Portugal (pousadas.pt) Official booking site for Grupo Pestana's monument and historic hotels.

Pousadas de Juventude (pousadasjuventude.pt) Official booking site for youth hostels.

Roteiro Campista (roteiro-campista.pt) Lists all the campsites in Portugal, including where to legally park campervans.

Termas de Portugal (termasdeportugal.pt) List of natural spas in Portugal. Some include accommodation and not all are open all year round.

CAMPING SITES

Camping options range from simple sites with modest facilities to complexes of permanent campervans, often by a beach and crowded in the summer. Prices start at around €10 per person and per tent or campervan.

ESSENTIAL NUTS-AND-BOLTS

NAVIGATION

Rely on GPS to avoid getting lost on backroads when road-tripping in Portugal. On foot, don't take suggestions for granted and observe your surroundings.

SMOKING

Smoking, including e-cigarettes, is not allowed in public spaces, except within designated areas. Most restaurants and cafes don't have a smoking section.

EMERGENCIES

Call 112.
For non-urgent situations, call SNS24 (808 24 24 24; press 9 for English).

FAST FACTS

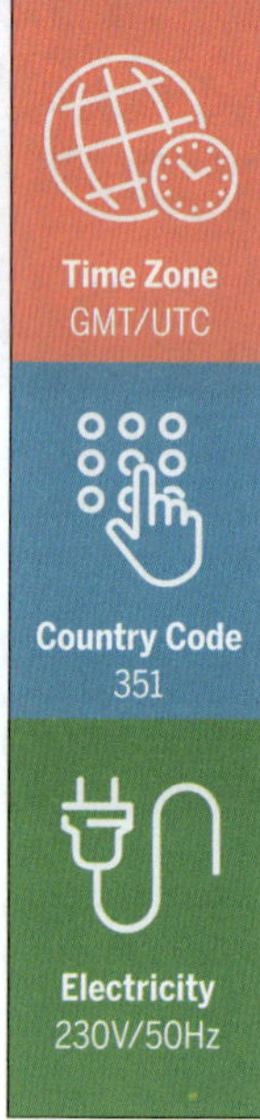

Time Zone
GMT/UTC

Country Code
351

Electricity
230V/50Hz

GOOD TO KNOW

If there's a queue, respect it and apologise if you unintentionally cut in line.

If you're carrying large luggage, opt for a ride-share or taxi instead of public transport.

The legal drinking age in Portugal is 18 and it's legal to drink in public.

EU and Schengen area citizens don't need a visa, just a valid ID.

Citizens of 60+ countries can travel to Portugal without a visa (vistos.mne.gov.pt).

ACCESSIBLE TRAVEL

Larger chain hotels will have wheelchair-friendly rooms; check before booking at smaller accommodations.

Main train and metro stations have lifts, though they're few or poorly located.

Cities' historic centres aren't wheelchair- or visually-impaired-friendly. Slippery, poorly maintained cobblestones and narrow streets make it difficult to navigate.

Braille descriptions are available at most museums and public services.

Accessible beach award honours beaches and other swimming areas for their wheelchair-friendly facilities. As of now, more than 200 places are certified.

tur4all.pt is a global, official resource for accessible travel in Portugal. You can also download the app for iOS and Android.

PUBLIC HOLIDAYS

There are 13 public holidays in Portugal. Some businesses and non-essential services may be closed.

BORDER CROSSING

Foreign nationals arriving in Portugal via an EU member state not subject to border control, such as Spain, must submit a Declaration of Entry within three days of arrival. This form is available on the SEF website (www.sef.pt).

PUBLIC TOILETS

In major cities, public toilets are scarce. Shopping centres, markets and cafes (customers only) are your best bet.

VACCINATIONS

Not mandatory for visiting Portugal, unless you're travelling from a Yellow Fever Zone.

FAMILY TRAVEL

Reduced fares for public transport, museums and attractions are available for children under 10 or 12.

Traditional trams are too narrow for strollers.

Kids' menus are more frequent at chain restaurants. At more traditional spots, ask if they can make something not on the menu, order a *meia dose* (half portion) or ask to bring your own food.

High chairs are available at most restaurants.

Child seats aren't available in taxis. If hiring a car, request one in advance.

LGBTIQ+ TRAVELLERS

Outright discrimination is unusual (or unreported), but outside major urban and touristic areas (Lisbon, Porto, Algarve) same-sex couples are still seen as outside the norm.

Lisbon has the largest gay scene. Gay communities are more discreet elsewhere.

Same-sex marriage has been legal in Portugal since 2010.

Law of Gender Identity, passed in 2011, allows transgender people to legally change their gender on official documents.

ILGA is an NGO assisting the LGBTIQ+ community. Check ilga-portugal.pt for updated reports and support groups.

LANGUAGE

Portuguese pronunciation is not difficult because most sounds are also found in English. The exceptions are the nasal vowels (represented in our pronunciation guides by ng after the vowel), which are pronounced as if you're trying to make the sound through your nose; and the strongly rolled r (represented by rr in our pronunciation guides). Also note that the symbol zh sounds like the 's' in 'pleasure'. In our pronunciation guides stressed syllables are indicated with italics.

To enhance your trip with a phrasebook, visit shop.lonelyplanet.com.

BASICS

Hello.	*Olá.*	o·*laa*
Goodbye.	*Adeus.*	a·de·*oosh*
Yes.	*Sim.*	seeng
No.	*Não.*	nowng
Please.	*Por favor.*	poor fa·*vor*
Thank you.	*Obrigado.*	o·bree·*gaa*·doo (m) o·bree·*gaa*·da (f)
You're welcome.	*De nada.*	de *naa*·da
Excuse me.	*Faz favor.*	faash fa·*vor*
Sorry.	*Desculpe.*	desh·*kool*·pe

What's your name?
Qual é o seu nome? kwaal e oo *se*·oo *no*·me

My name is ...
O meu nome é ... oo *me*·oo *no*·me e ...

Do you speak English?
Fala inglês? faa·la eeng·*glesh*

I don't understand.
Não entendo. nowng eng·*teng*·doo

TIME & NUMBERS

What time is it?	*Que horas são?*	kee *o*·rash sowng
It's (10) o'clock.	*São (dez) horas.*	sowng (desh) *o*·rash
Half past (10).	*(Dez) e meia.*	(desh) e *may*·a
morning	*manhã*	ma·*nyang*
afternoon	*tarde*	*taar*·de
evening	*noite*	*noy*·te
yesterday	*ontem*	*ong*·teng
today	*hoje*	*o*·zhe
tomorrow	*amanhã*	aa·ma·*nyang*

1	*um*	oong	**6**	*seis*	saysh
2	*dois*	doysh	**7**	*sete*	*se*·te
3	*três*	tresh	**8**	*oito*	*oy*·too
4	*quatro*	*kwaa*·troo	**9**	*nove*	*no*·ve
5	*cinco*	*seeng*·koo	**10**	*dez*	desh

EMERGENCIES

Help!	*Socorro!*	soo·*ko*·rroo
Go away!	*Vá-se embora!*	*vaa*·se eng·*bo*·ra
I'm ill.	*Estou doente.*	shtoh doo·*eng*·te
Call ...!	*Chame ...!*	*shaa*·me ...
a doctor	*um médico*	oong *me*·dee·koo
the police	*a polícia*	a poo·*lee*·sya

Index

000 Map pages

F

G

H

I

K

L

000 Map pages

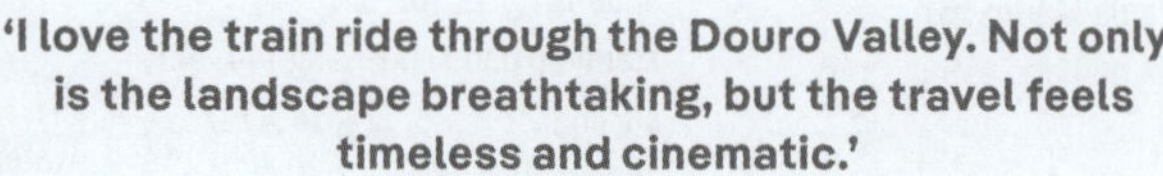

'I love the train ride through the Douro Valley. Not only is the landscape breathtaking, but the travel feels timeless and cinematic.'

GAIL AGUIAR

'My favourite thing is stumbling upon something unexpected – a postage stamp-sized garden, a centuries-old convent – as I'm out running an errand.'

JENNY BARCHFIELD

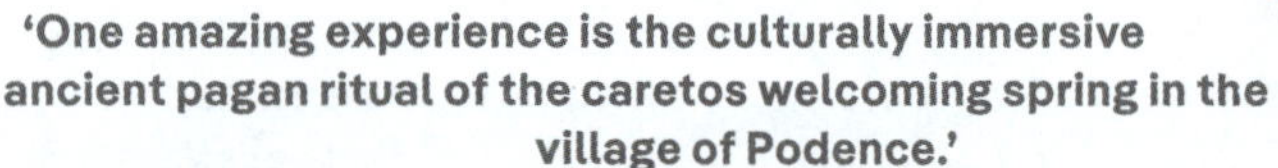

'My first zest for Portugal was aged five, when a kind-faced farmer handed me an Algarvian orange, a story that blossomed into a relocation.'

DANIEL JAMES CLARKE

'One amazing experience is the culturally immersive ancient pagan ritual of the caretos welcoming spring in the village of Podence.'

SANDRA HENRIQUES

'I love seeing paintings transformed into large, vibrant hand-woven tapestries at the Portalegre Tapestry Museum in Alentejo.'

JOANA TABORDA

TOP: ARMANDO OLIVEIRA/SHUTTERSTOCK ©, BOTTOM: VITOR_BRANDAO/SHUTTERSTOCK ©

THIS BOOK

Destination editor
AnneMarie McCarthy

Production editor
Vicky Smith

Cartographer
Bohumil Ptáček

Book designer
Catalina Aragón

Assisting editors
Janet Austin, Peterjon Cresswell, Shauna Daly

Cover researcher
Kat Marsh

Thanks Melanie Dankel, Kate Mathews, Jenna Myers